graphic design school

graphic design school

A L A N   S W A N N

 VAN NOSTRAND REINHOLD
New York

Copyright © 1991 Quarto Publishing plc

ISBN 0-442-30423-4

Published in the United States of America by
Van Nostrand Reinhold
115 Fifth Avenue
New York, New York 10003

This book was designed and produced by
Quarto Publishing plc
The Old Brewery
6 Blundell Street
London N7 9BH

16 15 14 13 12 11 10 9 8 7 6 5 4 3 2

Library of Congress Cataloging in Publication Data

Swann, Alan, 1946-
    Graphic design school/Alan Swann.
        p.   cm.
    ISBN 0–442–30423–4
    1. Graphic arts – Study and teaching. 2. Commercial art - Study and
teaching. 3. Photography – Study and teaching. I Title.
NC845.S93 1990
741.G – dc20   90-43410   CIP

Senior Editor Cathy Meeus
Project Editor Carolyn King
Copy Editors Richard Dawes, Charles Foster

Designer Alan Swann

Picture Research Manager Joanna Wiese
Art Director Moira Clinch
Publishing Director Janet Slingsby

The author and Quarto would also like to thank the following for their help in the
preparation of this book: Paul Diner, John Fairbanks (Buckinghamshire
College of Higher Education), Anita Ruddell, Ian Simpson.

This book contains examples of graphic design work. These examples are
included for the purposes of criticism and review.

Typeset in Great Britain by Ampersand Typesetting (Bournemouth) Ltd
Manufactured in Hong Kong by Regent Publishing Services Ltd
Printed in China by Leefung Asco Printers Ltd

CONTENTS

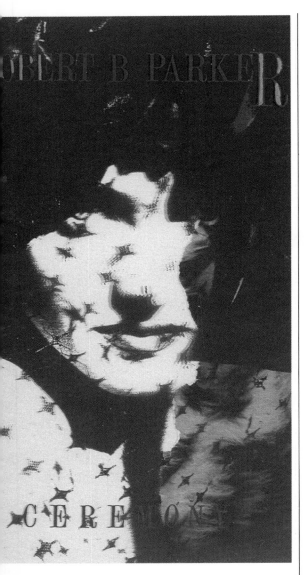

Above Book cover design by Samantha Bainbridge.

Author

ALAN SWANN has spent his entire working life in the field of art and design. Formerly a graphic designer with major newspapers and also an art director in advertising, he now lectures and writes extensively on design and design-related areas.

Contributors

IAN LOGAN trained as a textile designer at the Central School of Art and Design, London, following this up with further studies in Sweden. From relatively simple beginnings in the manufacture of household textiles and products, Ian Logan's design consultancy extended into packaging of toiletries and the designing and making of tins for the gift market. The Ian Logan Design Company and Massily Logan Limited are now very successful in the creation of giftware and tins and in the areas of food packaging, cosmetics packaging, corporate identity, catalogues and uniforms. Clients include Harrods, Waitrose and Perrier, Boots the Chemist, Filofax, the Post Office, and London Transport.

COLIN McHENRY obtained a graphic design degree at Saint Martin's School of Art in London, and then pursued an intensive one-year typography course at the London College of Printing. He spent four years as senior designer at the *Radio Times*, later moving to *Good Housekeeping* as art editor. He is currently Group Art Director at Centaur Publications, London.

PETER WINDETT studied printing and typography before joining *Vogue* magazine as a junior designer in 1965. From 1966-71 he worked in advertising, and set up his own design consultancy, concentrating principally on packaging design, and shop, restaurant and exhibition stand design for a number of major international clients, among them Crabtree & Evelyn, Penguin Books, Hediard (France), Scarborough & Co (USA), Glenmorangie Whisky, and Colefax & Fowler. He is the winner of numerous awards for art direction, including a gold award from the Art Directors' Club of New York in 1982.

BILLY MAWHINNEY joined J. Walter Thompson in 1978 as a trainee art director. After two years he returned to Belfast Art College, where he had trained, to take up a teaching post. He returned to JWT in 1982 to work with Alan Thomas, Executive Creative Director (and currently JWT's Chairman), and Max Henry then Head of Art. In 1985 he moved to Bartle, Bogle, Hegarty, but rejoined JWT in 1988 as Joint Creative Group Head with a place on the Board.

Advisors

The following designers have kindly given permission for individual student projects that they have devised, taught and supervised to appear in this book.

VICTORIA BENNETT (Program Director, Commercial Art/Graphics at The American College in London).

FRANCES BLOOMFIELD (Lecturer at Newham Community College, London).

PETER BURNS (Head of Course, Higher Diploma in Graphic Design, at Barnet College).

ALAN BUTTON (Part-time Lecturer in Graphic Design, Newham College and Croydon College and Graphic Design Consultant).

PHIL DUFFY (Head of Graphic Design at Epping College, Essex).

DAVID FERRY (Lecturer, Kent Institute of Art and Design).

SUE HERRON (Lecturer in Graphic Design, East Ham College, London).

ERNEST JONES (Visiting Lecturer, Croydon College).

MICHAEL SHEEDY (Lecturer, Newham Community College in London and Visiting Lecturer at the Kent Institute of Art and Design).

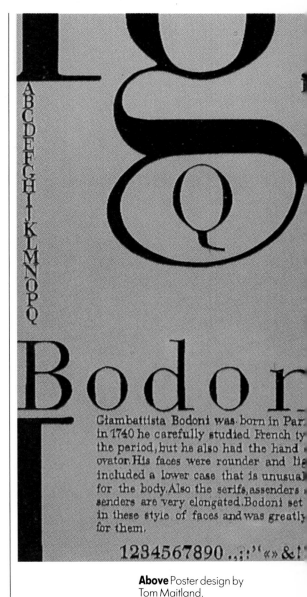

Above Poster design by Tom Maitland.

INTRODUCTION

This book shows how the basic principles of graphic design are currently taught and learned in art school courses. It uses real examples of students' work, so that the reader sees how a piece of design evolves, and can thereby become aware both of his or her own creative potential and the techniques necessary to put good design into practice.

Each project is shown step by step. In the beginning the reader is introduced to the process of looking and translating what is seen into drawings and designs. The use of different media is encouraged in order to find their expressive qualities. Each area of work develops the reader's individual way of thinking and interpreting visual ideas.

The early part of the book is deliberately structured to show the natural talent of the featured students. Projects were chosen that allowed freedom of expression and individual interpretation. This is to demonstrate how important it is for the graphic designer to experience the joy of creating images in the way he or she wants to present them. I hope to fire your enthusiasm by encouraging your free expression here. At the same time you should learn how to control the available media.

The middle section of the book leads the reader into how to solve graphic design problems. This is explored through a number of projects in which visual ideas are evolved. The students demonstrate their ability to research solutions and resolve problems with ideas that communicate in both an original and effective manner.

Successful graphic design needs careful planning and research before ideas are explored. Approaching a problem without knowledge or preparation will not solve it. You need to use every available source of visual reference, including a sound knowledge of the historical development of images, as well as an awareness of contemporary trends.

The book demonstrates the gradual process needed to arrive at a commercially successful graphic design. At this point you will begin to know the kinds of work you wish to undertake, having discovered that advertising is a different discipline from, say, packaging. You may choose to develop your illustrative abilities, or to specialize in typography. Whatever your specialty, creative abilities are constantly in demand.

The last section of the book not only offers you the experience of seeing how students have developed commercial projects under guidance by teachers, but also provides a unique insight into the four main areas of graphic design. Introductions to each of these areas are provided by top professionals.

Whatever your reason for opening this book, it is my sincere hope that through it you gain an insight into the visual world of the graphic designer.

Alan Swann.

Chapter One: THE LANGUAGE OF DESIGN

Sight is a process by which our brains decode the visual stimuli received from the eyes and turn these into an image of solid objects in three-dimensional space. To learn to express yourself visually, you have to learn to see, rather than just use the sense of sight.

The artist Matisse said that when he ate a tomato, he just looked at it. "But," he added, "when I paint a tomato, I see it differently." And so it is for designers, who must develop a heightened awareness of the way the world looks.

But how can they do this? For many years, students struggled along in life classes, learning to draw. The idea was that by looking, analyzing, and translating what they had seen into marks on paper they would acquire visual skills and experience. This they could then use when conceptualizing a design. But the problem was that often the life class did not teach students to see – it merely equipped them with the skills and short cuts necessary to produce impressive life drawings.

Drawing was then deemed unnecessary for a while, and a lot of design students graduated who had hardly ever drawn at all. Attitudes have changed now again, partly because of the popularity nowadays of

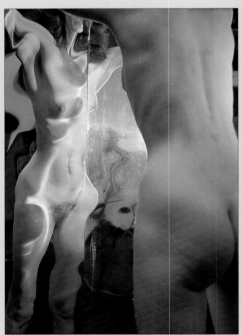

■ **Above** Experimental figure studies develop the ability to "see".

representational images in design. But it had also been noticed that designers who never developed the special way of seeing required for drawing were severely handicapped.

So how do we learn to see like an artist? I know of no formal way of teaching someone except by some form of training to draw. But this basic training can be expanded by visual research — looking for the extraordinary in the ordinary. For example, placing an object in an unusual position — a stool upside down, say — forces you to look more closely at it. Because it is no longer in its everyday mode, your awareness of what it really is, how it really looks, is increased.

But is drawing the only way in which we can expand our ability to see? There are certainly some designers of distinction who can't draw. These may be likened to those gifted people who learn to play the piano by ear. For most of the rest of us there is no alternative but a bit of hard work.

Once you have learned this active seeing, you are able to draw anything you can really see. And that's the way you can heighten your visual awareness, and through that your creativity.

Exploratory drawing: FORM AND SPACE

The purpose of exploratory drawing for the future graphic designer is to discover his or her personal expression through the images they are creating, for design work is based on such experimentation. Even in the early stages of this work, individual characteristics begin to emerge. Students approach the problem with their own capacity for interpretation: some prefer a calculated and mathematical route to solving a drawing problem, while others adopt the looser, more exploratory methods of describing form. The relevance of monochromatic drawing to graphic design is that it makes you see the subject as a shape or shapes and color as tones, teaches you to understand and manipulate perspective, and shows you how to convey texture and density. These skills are all necessary when designing in two dimensions for graphic reproduction, or indeed in three-dimensional package design.

It is also necessary for students to experiment beyond their own territory, attempting to achieve a full understanding of as many kinds of visual interpretation as possible and the methods by which they are created.

The first step in learning this new language of drawing is to set up a situation that allows you to explore the principles of looking and seeing. Many exercises can be used to initiate this process, which should begin with discovering visual information and then transferring it to paper.

Regardless of the level of attainment in drawing, it is essential to start at the beginning. Even students with considerable natural drawing ability must view this language as something to be learned anew. They may already be able to interpret objects and structures in a skillful way but with a narrow vision. There is an analogy with a spoken language. Most native speakers of a language are reasonably fluent in communication, yet lack a true understanding of the grammar

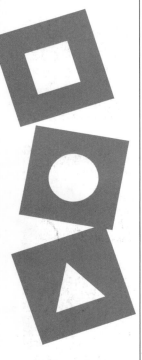

■ **Making a viewing device** is a simple way of isolating the area to be drawn. It can be cut from stiff gray or black board in various sizes and shapes.

MONOCHROME STILL-LIFE EXERCISE

Set up a still-life including as many different materials, shapes, sizes, and tonal objects as possible. Try to include both straight-edged and curved objects. Any objects will do – they could be discarded items. First experiment with the drawing media to see the marks they make. Next, select a number of media with which to create the first drawing. Make a line drawing of part of the still-life, experimenting with different kinds of lines. The next stage is to draw a series of selected line observations viewed through a cut-out shape or viewer. Next, through your viewer, take part of the still-life and make a pencil line drawing of the objects. Decide where there is space and where there is a solid object. Paint the solids in black, leaving the spaces white. Now do this exercise again, exchanging black for white.

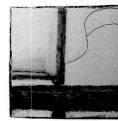

■ **Experimental mark-making** The quality and impact of a drawing are controlled by the pressure exerted on the instrument and the shape of its point.

and structure of their language. By contrast, someone who has learned a second language has had to gain a deep knowledge of how to pronounce it, how to structure sentences, and how to use the language according to its rules. In a similar way, by understanding the structure and grammar of drawing you can control the images you create in a decisive and planned manner. By being able to control the visual message of your work you can make drawing an exciting skill. Drawing becomes the basis of all future expression and underpins all your design decisions.

Observation

The first project focuses on the essentials. It sets up a stationary structure, enabling you to become familiar with all aspects of the forms it comprises. Having set up a group of still-life objects, you can explore them from various angles. Spend time sitting and viewing what is in front of you, taking account of the shapes and tonal forms. Move around and take up a fresh position, again just viewing the forms before you. Once you are familiar with what you see, the first mark-making can take place. The term "mark-making" is used because your first awareness should be of the instruments and the marks you will make with them on the paper.

For all these drawings, experiment with different media to assist the process of seeing and contemplating (see pages 22-23). Each of the media – whether charcoal or pencil, crayon or brush – will condition both the method you use and the image you create. Each instrument you use requires some understanding, as some can be used only for a specific effect. For instance, pencils, with their wide range of grades, from hard to soft, allow tonal control and detailed modeling. Not only the grade of pencil, but also the way it is sharpened will determine the kind of marks you make. Naturally, a

■ **Space frame** A random arrangement of unrelated material (left) within a framework or scaffold will stimulate experimental drawings.

■ **Negative and positive shapes** An outline drawing of the shapes within a section of the still-life set-up (below). The shapes have been filled in ink.

■ **Alternative space** Look at the still-life set-up from different angles with the viewing frame, and reverse the shapes, making the objects white and filling in the spaces between them with charcoal or ink (above).

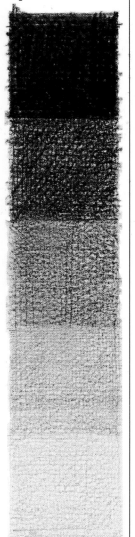

finely sharpened instrument creates only a finely produced line.

Charcoal and chalk should be used to make other kinds of marks. But this process of discovery should not be limited just to traditional media, for even a discarded toothbrush or string can be used to define tonal contrasts or linear forms.

Bear in mind all the time that you are looking for inspirational leads from your objects to assist you in learning to understand what you see. The aim is not merely to interpret the objects in a pictorial way, although clearly they need to be drawn with some accuracy to allow a first assessment of the complexities of the form before you. Then, once an initial drawing has evolved, analysis of it should follow. It is natural for most students to place a line on the paper and use this line to form the object. But it is a common fault to consider that line as sacrosanct and permanent.

Understanding form

There are no lines around objects unless they have been deliberately printed on the outer edges. Objects consist of their own form and the light that falls upon them. It is tone that defines them. The normal process is to create black and white drawings. It is right to do this, but understand that you are abstracting from real life and translating the language of color into tone, substituting tones for the complexity of a range of colors.

Once you are aware that the line does not exist in reality, it no longer matters that, when you draw, a single line is used to describe one surface. Also, the media themselves are an abstraction, for while you may be drawing a plastic bowl in, say, charcoal, this medium has nothing to do with plastic. Yet charcoal is perfectly valid as a modeling tool. If charcoal can be used to represent a

plastic object, then why not try representing that same object in pieces of string, or cutout cardboard, or anything that enables you to express visually what you see?

You will now begin to realize the importance of understanding how to control the images you are creating. A good test for all students of how accurate and concentrated a drawing can be is to set about making a drawing that is wholly in line. A great deal of skill is needed to do this accurately, as all the planes and surfaces of the objects have to be understood in terms of their form to create a good line representation. Even the unexposed surfaces need to be realized on paper. Most people make the mistake in objective drawing of creating a stripped-down version of reality.

Negative and positive forms

You can use the same still-life arrangement to try many forms of discovery. It is usual to identify the objects and make a drawing of these within the space they occupy. Another means of identifying the form is to look for the negative shape – that is, the space that is not occupied by the objects.

Take the objects themselves and consider the space between them as a solid form. A good medium for this is ink and brush, with which the spaces can just be painted out, forming a solid negative design. The same process can be tried in a number of media. In another exercise the objects are drawn and painted using black as a solid color. A tone halfway between black and white is used to depict the areas of the object that are halfway between the lightest and darkest parts. The lightest parts are left white, creating a pattern of shapes that range from white to medium tone to black. This early work starts to make you aware of flat shapes within a space which create a composition.

■ **Tonal drawing** A portion of the still-life has been selected in the viewing frame and rendered using the full range of tones to create a tonal drawing made up of interesting interlocking shapes. Mixing the media also gives a pleasing contrast.

DISCOVERING FORM AND TONE
EXERCISE

Looking through your viewer, choose part of a still-life and make a pencil line drawing of the objects. Decide where there is space and where there is a solid object. Decide which areas of the objects are dark and which have a lighter tone. Leave the space white, paint the lighter tones in gray, and paint the dark areas in black.

Create a series of tonal scales ranging from white to black. Do this in pencil, charcoal, black and white Conté, inks, paint, or using different tones of newsprint. Select a portion of the still-life and create a tonal drawing, expressing some aspect of the set-up.

■ **Black, white, and gray** A drawing of a section of the still-life (page 13) with tones applied in gouache to identify the subject in terms of dark, medium, and light areas.

15

Exploratory drawing: COMPOSITION

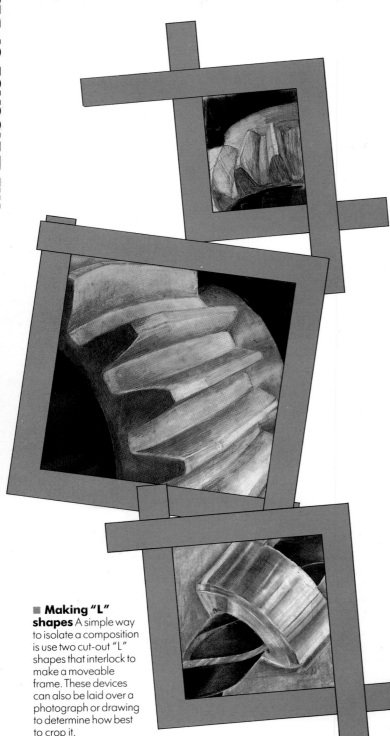

■ **Making "L" shapes** A simple way to isolate a composition is use two cut-out "L" shapes that interlock to make a moveable frame. These devices can also be laid over a photograph or drawing to determine how best to crop it.

You cannot produce a successful piece of work without giving consideration to its composition. Throughout the history of the visual arts different theories of composition have been advanced. Vitruvius, the Roman architect and engineer, devised a mathematical formula for the division of space within a picture. His solution, known as the Golden Section and sometimes as the Golden Mean, was based on a set ratio between the longer sides and the shorter sides of a rectangle. The French painter Henri Matisse (1869-1954) put greater emphasis on inspiration, maintaining that composition is the art of arranging the various elements so as to express feelings in a decorative fashion. The key notion is elements expressing feelings.

To produce a composition from a still-life arrangement you need either to rearrange the objects within the space or to find the right perspective in which to see them. The first option is the easier, in that you can arrange the objects to create any shape, form, or mood. The second approach requires you to move around the object or objects to find a position that has the potential for making an interesting composition.

As we have seen on page 12, you can also cut out shapes – circles, rectangles, squares, triangles, or irregular shapes – from black illustration board to make viewing instruments. With the viewer to your eye, you can move it further away or closer to you to see more or less of the subject matter in front of you. Or you can use two "L" shapes cut out of card as a moveable frame (see left).

Perspective

To create a convincing drawing a knowledge of perspective is essential. Perspective is simply a way of representing three-dimensional objects on a two-dimensional surface. To produce an accurate impression of three-dimensional objects in the space they occupy, and to represent these on a two-dimensional surface, maintaining their correct spatial relationships, requires a set of formulas.

Once these simple rules are understood, you can manipulate the three-dimensional space represented in your composition. For example, a large building can be arranged in such a way that it is dominated by a single person in front of it.

Another consideration is what is known as aerial perspective. Not only does an object become less defined as it recedes into the background but it also changes its tonal value. To relate this phenomenon to color, a bright red in the foreground is changed beyond recognition when placed in the background.

PERSPECTIVE EXERCISE

Take a cube and view it from three different perspectives. First, a one-point perspective directly behind the cube. Second, draw in a horizontal line that represents the level of your eye, and draw the cube in two-point perspective. Next, put in your eye-level again, and this time draw in three points of perspective.

For the next exercise take a cylinder. Draw a square on your page. Find the center by drawing in the diagonals. Take the central point, and with a compass draw in a circle to fit inside the square exactly. Draw another square inside the circle. From your previous exercises with the cube you know how to draw the cube in perspective. Apply this knowledge to the circle (within a square) to produce ellipses. To create a cylinder, join up the ellipses and rub out the lines making up the squares. Finally create a drawing using all the perspective techniques you have acquired.

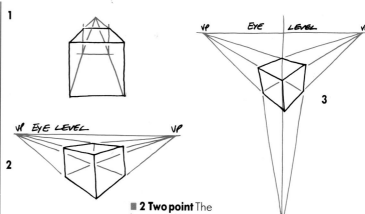

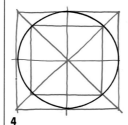

■ **1 One point** Lines drawn from a single vanishing point (VP), will give you a simple box shape.

■ **4 Plan an ellipse** by following the diagram, drawing a circle and then adding a square to it, both inside and outside the circle.

■ **5 Ellipse** First draw a rectangle in perspective using the measurements from **4**. To make an ellipse, draw in the diagonals and the inner box shape, following all the perspective lines. With the squares and diagonals as reference points, the ellipse can now be drawn in. Do this to both ends of the

■ **2 Two point** The horizontal line represents your eye level. With two vanishing points, the sides of a cube can be constructed accurately in perspective. The elevations differ, however, according to where the cube is placed. The top of your cube can be drawn once the size of the sides has been determined.

■ **3 Three point** The vertical line is drawn first, then the horizontal line marks the eye level. There are three vanishing points: two on the eye level and one at the bottom of the vertical. For the bottom of the cube, two lines are drawn first from a single point on the vertical – one to each of the vanishing points on the eye level. This is then repeated for the top of the cube. The sides of the cube are drawn from the bottom vanishing point.

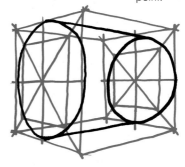

rectangle; parallel lines joining the two ellipses will then create a cylinder.

Exploratory drawing: THUMBNAILS

It is impossible, in the early stages of your studies, to create any finished piece of work without testing out your ideas first and rigorously putting these through a process of intensive investigation.

Before you begin to create your image you must go through a period of visual investigation in which you produce small, quick interpretations of the objects in front of you. These thumbnail sketches will help you decide on all the factors you are looking for in the work you wish to create. Use them to test out different compositions and tonal effects, in many techniques.

The more thoroughly this exploratory work is done the more ideas you will have to feed on when the work of producing a design begins. Your time should be spent seeing not only how the images respond to different layouts, but also how a different medium changes the impression of the actual subject itself. You should look for media that express the quality of the subjects you draw. You should discover different ways of expressing those images by setting time limits within which to work for each sketch. You can also try applying improvised media. For example, cotton dipped in ink and drawn on the surface produces a loose image. A charcoal-covered area can be drawn into by using a sharpened, hard eraser. Stencil brushes are useful for quick tonal effects. There is no end to the methods you can discover for yourself. The more inventive images you create, the closer you are to understanding the process of design.

Developing ideas from thumbnails

Once you have created a number of thumbnails, further development can begin. Look at them with a critical eye to discover their strengths and weaknesses. Find different visual themes in them, such as their dynamic or passive or dramatic force. Use your thumbnails to invent other compositions by incorporating the two themes into a single enlarged image. Control the tonal qualities again by using media that are sympathetic to the ideas you are trying to create. The skills you will gain from exploring media and becoming accomplished and confident in your interpretation will assist in the later development of your graphic design ability.

■ **Worksheets** represent a series of thought processes or ideas visualized on paper before lengthy designs or complex illustrations are begun. These images are known as thumbnail sketches (right) and they are essential to clarify and demonstrate the evolution of a piece of work.

EXPRESSIVE DRAWING **EXERCISE**

Take a simple object and draw a series of thumbnails to give yourself a range of alternative designs and compositions. Then make a series of developed drawings that express the material or structure of your object. See how many media you can mix to produce your expressive drawings. Also explore working in reverse, creating a black square of charcoal or ink and tonally lightening the drawn areas to form the object.

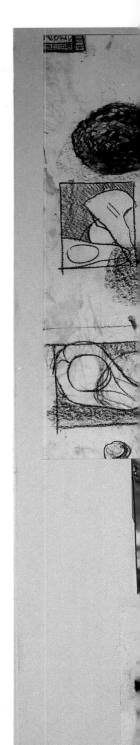

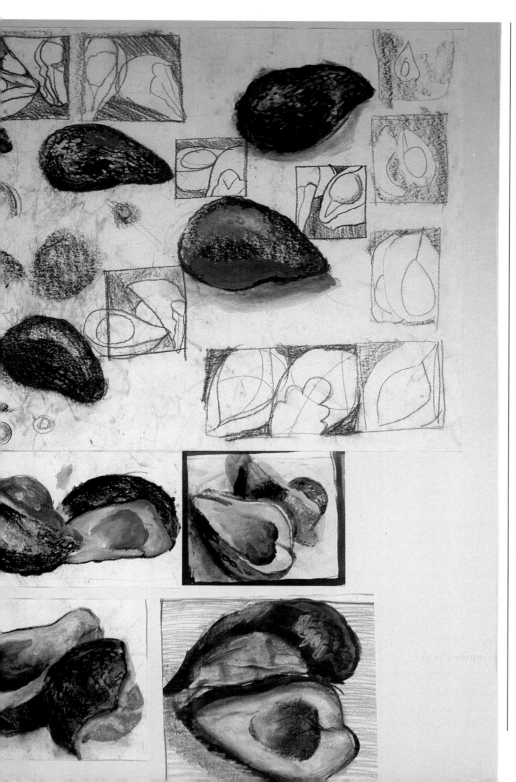

T I P S

■ Drawing is an opportunity to experiment with different media.

■ Drawings need not have photographic accuracy, but should be expressive and adventurous.

■ Treat your drawing as a design. Be selective in what you include.

■ Work out a tonal scale before producing tone drawings.

■ Tones can be created using any medium.

■ Mix media to help represent the form.

■ Work in reverse, creating light tones from solid black as an exercise.

■ Adjust the room lighting, if necessary, to assist in your drawing.

■ Always put down your eye-level line first.

■ Most geometric shapes can be fitted inside a cube.

■ Remember that an ellipse is a circle in perspective.

■ Always make a series of thumbnails first, and then use a selection of these to develop other drawings.

Exploratory drawing: STUDIES FROM LIFE

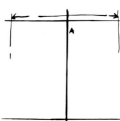

1 The middle line decides the actual size of the drawing, and the overall proportions and shape can be measured against this vertical.

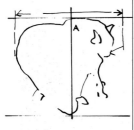

2 Next, the overall width of the subject is plotted, relating it to the vertical.

3 Indicate the shapes tonally, referring always to the middle line.

Life drawing is possibly the most testing form of drawing. Many people underestimate the difficulties of this task, as they come to it believing that their familiarity with the human form will make it easy. The first problem to be resolved is how you view the figure you are drawing. It is natural to want to draw around the shape of the figure, but this can result in disaster for two reasons. First, as with objects, there is no actual line around a human form. Second, the human form is made up of many shapes, and these each have a measurement that must be determined before drawing starts.

A formula for measurement

First, choose a medium suitable for drawing. Then, working from the center of the sitter's body, place a straight centre line through the body which follows the main route of the form. This line will also determine the size your drawing will be. From this you can work out the shapes on either side of the line (see illustrations left). To discover the position of the elements of the body put a dot on to your paper to represent a nipple. The next decision concerns the size your drawing will be. Position the second dot, representing the second nipple, on your paper, bearing in mind that, depending on the position of the sitter, the position of the dot may be above, level with, or below the first dot. The crucial factor is the distance between the two dots, as this determines the scale of your drawing. The closer together they are, the smaller your finished image will appear, and vice versa.

The next mark represents the navel. Its position is crucial, because it must be placed in the correct relationship to the two dots you have already made. You will now realize that each point of the body can be plotted in relation to these early measure-

ments. You may also have discovered that the navel is farther away from one nipple than the other. Because each point of the body you move on to will bear some relationship to these central measurements, it is important to get the first three points right.

You must view the body from the center of its main feature (the torso), because if you started by drawing around one foot you might draw a nicely proportioned foot, but you would not be able to control the size and proportion of the whole drawing, and you would soon lose sight of the proportional relationship of each member of the body. It is best to measure the parts of the body and compare these dimensions. For example, how many heads fit in a torso? How many heads equal the upper part of the leg, or the lower?

Do not expect to make an elegant drawing at this stage. This drawing should just be a series of marks. The purpose of this exercise is understanding how to draw. You can use your skills in tone and color once you understand better the proportions of individual parts of the body.

By drawing lines between your marks, you will begin to establish the flow of the shapes of the body. When you are familiar with the marks you have made and are happy with how they relate to each other, you need to measure the form of the body.

Measuring the form

Think of the body as a series of cylinders. Establish the volume of each part of the body, again by measuring and placing dots spaced proportionally as reference points. The cylinders will indicate the volume of different parts of the body. The contours of the body itself will then need to be modeled into these cylindrical shapes.

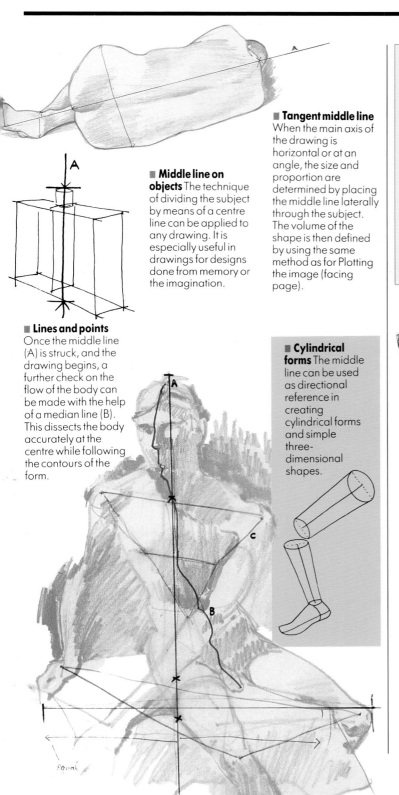

■ Middle line on objects

The technique of dividing the subject by means of a centre line can be applied to any drawing. It is especially useful in drawings for designs done from memory or the imagination.

■ Lines and points

Once the middle line (A) is struck, and the drawing begins, a further check on the flow of the body can be made with the help of a median line (B). This dissects the body accurately at the centre while following the contours of the form.

■ Tangent middle line

When the main axis of the drawing is horizontal or at an angle, the size and proportion are determined by placing the middle line laterally through the subject. The volume of the shape is then defined by using the same method as for Plotting the image (facing page).

■ Cylindrical forms

The middle line can be used as directional reference in creating cylindrical forms and simple three-dimensional shapes.

ZOO STUDIES EXERCISE

Study an animal or group of animals. Understand their proportions and their form. Make thumbnail sketches depicting their form and structure. Using these drawings, create more drawings which express something of the characteristics of the animal. Experiment with different media to create textures and tones that serve to express your own feeling about the creature.

Develop the first set of drawings further, combining them with the memory of what you saw.

■ Sketchbook notes

Observational drawings as a preparation for studio work should be carried out thoroughly, speedily and accurately.

■ **Developing drawings** Using the sketchbook drawings, further techniques can be explored. This gorilla profile was created as a simple mono print. Printing ink was spread on a sheet of thick glass and drawn into.

■ **Unusual media** can be used to make effective marks. For example, in this gorilla's face, shoe polish was applied with a toothbrush and ink with a finger.

Once you are familiar with the structure of the body, you can then start the drawing process of creating the volumes in tone and color. As with the exercises based on white and black objects, study the form carefully for the subtle surprises in color to be found. You will find parts of the body will be picking up blues and greens, and you will need the same range of colors in depicting your subject as you used in the still-life project.

Making drawings of this kind will help you understand proportion in your graphic design work. It is not necessary for the graphics student to excel in life drawing, but it should be attempted seriously, as it will make it easier to produce good visuals from memory later on.

Texture and surface

Now you have gained some confidence, it is time to experiment with different media to achieve a sense of the texture or characteristics of the subject.

Experiments can now be made with charcoal, gouache, inks, and other media. You should now see your subjects in terms of more than just their visual measurements. How, for example, would you depict the

■ **From sketch to print** A simple print can be produced by starting with a drawing from life, then rolling ink on a glass sheet and drawing over it into the ink.

■ **Mono print** By placing paper against the ink, you can transfer the image onto the paper. Multi-colored pictures are made by selectively arranging colored inks on the surface of the glass.

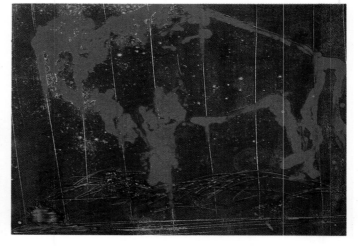

texture and surface of different living creatures? The smooth porcelain-like form of a human baby would be rendered differently from that of, say, a baby gorilla.

You should be prepared to try out all kinds of media, singly and in combination, to depict different materials. For example, try to depict the feeling of coarse fur in charcoal. Or ink sponged on the surface, both dry and wet? Do pastel and colored pencil mix with charcoal to create a sense of weight? Try drawing the same subject in different media to discover which captures the essence of the subject in the most dynamic way.

It is essential to the graphic designer to be able to make drawings based on a memory of subjects and objects. It is from this visual fund that he or she conjures up a range of images that will help resolve a design problem.

■ **Draw the object you see** The illustration above expresses the image realistically. Select media that express the color, tone, and texture to maximum effect, experimenting to achieve the desired results.

■ **Drawing and the imagination** Become familiar with the forms of real objects, and then try to see and draw them in more imaginative ways, rather than totally realistically. Experiment with familiar media to develop an individual style or way of working.

Select an object and try to understand its structure by making detailed studies of it while it is in front of you. Then use the drawing and your memory of the object to create more drawings. Put down your own ideas of the object's shape and form and see what images and designs you can evolve. Allow color to affect your visual decisions, and play around with colors to change the appearance of the design itself. You can take this exercise further and create realistic or stylized drawings. Make it a regular practice to sit and study the shape of an object. Then without reference to the object, make a drawing of it; compare the result with the object itself.

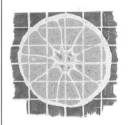

■ **Designs from the object** By using the basic form of the object, patterns and shapes can emerge which are much more stylized.

Learning about colour: BASIC PRINCIPLES

■ **The ruling pen** is a valuable piece of equipment for achieving accurate lines in colored ink or water-soluble paint such as gouache. With its adjustable action, lines of any thickness can be drawn.

1 Adjust the pen using the screw.

2 Ensure that the points are not touching.

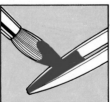

3 Mix the paint or ink to the correct consistency and load it between the points with a brush.

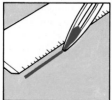

4 Run the pen along the edge of a plastic set square or ruler, bevel edge down.

Color plays an important part in making graphic design decisions. It is therefore important for the designer to be aware of how colors mix with one another to produce other colors. All colors are made up of three basic components – red, yellow, and blue. By mixing pairs of these so-called primary colors you can produce another range of basic colors, known as the secondaries. Further mixing of two of these secondaries in different proportions produces an intermediate range. Finally, the tertiary colors can be mixed by adding different percentages of all three of the primaries.

Besides mixing colors together, you can add white to lighten or black to darken the result, creating what is known as tints of color (adding white) and shades of color (adding black). Three other properties of color with which you should be familiar are hue, value, and intensity. Hue is what distinguishes one color from another. In effect it is the generic name of the color – red, for example, is a different hue from blue. However, there are different types of red, and these are distinguished by their value and intensity. Value is the word used to identify the amount of light or dark within a color, while intensity, which is also referred to as color saturation or chroma, is roughly speaking the equivalent of brightness. For example, a hue of high intensity is a bright color, while one of low intensity is a dull color. Two reds can be of the same hue but have different intensities.

It is important to note that black and white have no intensity and are therefore classified as having zero hue. However, because black and white can have value, from white through grays, to black, they can be used to measure the value of hues.

Much color theory was developed by Johannes Itten, who was a teacher of color at the Bauhaus in Germany in the 1920s. The Bauhaus is of great importance to graphic design for its dedication to design, and its influence is still apparent in the field today.

The student of design should also consider how colors suggest heat or coldness. This is

THE COLOUR WHEEL EXERCISE

As an initial exercise, produce a color wheel to see how colors can be mixed. You will need to use designer's gouache, which enables you to lay a flat, opaque color. However, care should be taken to mix this paint to the right consistency. Unlike watercolor, this paint should have a creamy quality. Add only enough water to make the mix easy to apply.

You will need a palette with many pans. Mix up the pure yellow, pure red, and pure blue to a workable consistency. Test your mix by applying it to a piece of scrap paper. With gouache you do not need to stretch your drawing paper if your mix is correct.

Use a pencil and compass to draw a neat circle of 6in (15cm) in diameter with 12 equal segments. Paint the first of your primary colors into one of these segments. Move around the circle, leaving the next three segments clear, and in the fourth segment paint in the next primary. Leave another three segments clear and paint in your third primary.

To create the secondary color, mix your first primary equally with your second primary and paint in this mix between the two colors already in position, in the middle segment. Repeat this exercise with the next mix of primaries and again with the third mix. You have now created the three secondary colors. You should now have six painted segments and six blank. The painted segments lie in the order: primary, secondary, primary, secondary, primary, secondary. Between each painted segment is a blank segment.

To create the intermediate colors, mix equal proportions of the primary and secondary colors which surround a blank segment, and fill that segment with the resulting color.

A   B   C

■ **Primaries** The three basic colors – red, yellow and blue.

1   2   3

■ **Secondaries** are achieved with an equal mixture of two of the three primaries.
1 = A + B
2 = B + C
3 = C + A

4   5   6

■ **Intermediate colors** are created by mixing two primaries in a ratio of 2:1.
4 = 2A + B
5 = 2B + A
6 = 2B + C

7   8   9

7 = 2A + C
8 = 2C + A
9 = 2C + B

10   11   12

■ **Tertiaries** are created by mixing the three primaries together in different percentages.
10 = 2A + B + C
11 = 2B + A + C
12 = 2C + A + B

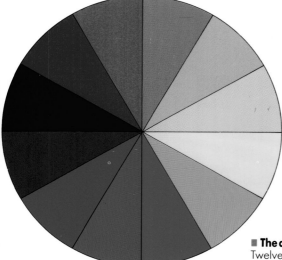

■ **The color wheel** Twelve segments displaying the primaries, secondaries and intermediates. The ruling pen divides each segment neatly.

■ **Designs in color** in which the individual colors overlap to show how they interlink. The first design (top) has been worked out roughly in colored pencil, quickly establishing the potential positions of the colors. Above, gouache mixtures test the different qualities of this medium with its more precise color mixing. Using the earlier roughs, a finished design (left) painted in gouache is bold and confident, and cleanly presented with the help of a ruling pen.

25

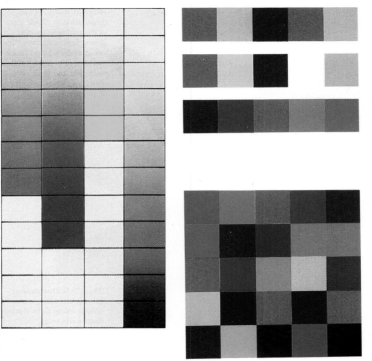

■ **Color value** is the quality or amount of light or dark held by the color. The grey scale is shown from light to dark. Beside it are the scales for red, blue and yellow, and their positions in relation to the grey scale. The blue is darker in value than the yellow and therefore descends further down the scale.

■ **Color intensity** The three bars of color show hue, value, and intensity. The top bar of five colors (left) gives the greatest contrast of hue. The middle bar shows the relationship between black and white and primaries, and demonstrates the effect black and white have on the intensity of hues: white adjacent to a color makes the color look darker; black intensifies color, so giving the effect of lightening the color. The bottom bar is made up of colors of the greatest intensity. A checkerboard (below left) can be made out of the colors of greatest intensity, providing an almost consistent brightness.

perhaps obvious in the case of red and orange, which are essentially warm colors, or the opposite scale of blue and green, which suggest coldness. It becomes more difficult to determine this effect the more subtle the hue becomes. It is therefore important to calculate the temperature of your color remembering that color itself has an emotional effect on the viewer, even though he or she may not be aware of it.

Harmony and discord

Once you have established the range of colors available to you and you are in control of their hue, value, and intensity, you can manipulate a design to give it a particular emphasis. For example, your colors may be harmonious, creating a pleasant and comfortable feeling. Or, if you wish to stress tension in your design, you can juxtapose colors that create a visual imbalance and a feeling of discomfort or discord.

Special effects can be created with color, and a good example is when two complementary colors are displayed in equal proportions to create a color balance. Complementary colors are those found facing one another on the color wheel – for example, blue and orange, red and green.

The choice of media for creating color is wide. To produce color mixes, though, and understand the creation of various colors, it is best to use a wet medium. The one that gives you the most scope is designer's gouache. This is an opaque medium that allows you to mix precisely the color you

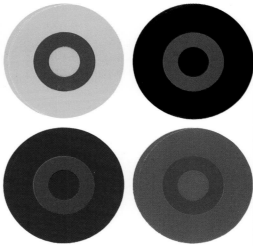

■ Color relationships In each of these four illustrations the blue inner circle is set on a different color background. Although the blue is identical in each case, it appears different when combined with each of the other colors.

■ Color squares The squares (below) have all been drawn to equal proportions yet appear different in size as a result of the optical effect that two adjacent colors have on one another.

■ Special effects The grid shows complementaries of equal proportion and therefore of equal strength. The effect this produces is of changing patterns, each one temporarily taking a dominant role.

require without its being affected by the color of the surface to which it is applied. However, for most designs you will be more likely to use colored markers or pencils in the initial stage for speed of image-making. Colored markers are available that correspond to the colors printers are able to mix, so that at a very early stage you can select colors that can be reproduced accurately.

Although printing methods and, in particular, printing color have a greater effect on later projects, pages 84-85, you should nevertheless be aware in your earliest work of how your mixing of color relates to that of the printer. The printer uses inks in three primary colors – cyan (blue), yellow, and magenta (red) – and these are mixed at different proportions on the surface of the

paper to create a full range of colors. Black is added to give the color modeling and paper with extra whiteness is used to lighten the effect where appropriate.

Learning about color : EXPERIMENTATION

Once you are familiar with the theory of color, you need to identify how colors work in reality. To become aware that color itself is not just the product of the surface color or "local" color of an object, some exploration is essential. Light itself, in all its natural variations, affects what you are seeing. The ever-changing quality of natural light makes subject matter undergo a constant metamorphosis of color. In bright sunlight an object clearly looks different from how it appears in evening light, but the subtle changes in lighting conditions that occur at every moment of the day produce an infinite range of effects.

We are generally unaware of such changes unless we see a photographic sequence recording their effect at different times of day. Being conscious of the effects of color can play an important part in your design work and also assist in the development of a photographic and illustrative eye. Once aware of the subtle change in the value of your colors, forced on the subject matter either by natural changes in daylight or by artificial light, you can begin to control it in your work and use it to creative effect.

The following exercises have been devised to allow you to interpret the colors of a set of similarly colored objects. The way to test observational skill and enhance your knowledge of mixing color is to set a series of black objects on a black background. Experiment with interpreting the objects in a black medium and you will find that the result does not reflect the true range of color in the objects. This is because the colored light on their surface creates a much richer range than can be depicted by using black on its own, or even by adding white.

Once pure black is eliminated, dark colors can be created by mixing together colors which are opposite one another on the color wheel. Browns and blues offer a greater range for depicting the colors you see in the objects.

With white objects on a white background the task becomes even subtler, as the objects reflect, rather than, like black, absorb light. For instance, the color from a cloudless sky will be highly influential, but should the sky cloud over, the whole tonal range of your objects will be transformed. You can test this effect by filtering the light from the window with tracing paper or another diffusing material or by allowing natural light to reflect off strategically placed colors.

■ **Setting up** The objects below are more or less the same color, placed together to form a still-life. Any combination of colors is suitable for this exercise so long as they are all of the same hue.

STARTING WORK WITH COLOR
EXERCISE

Set up a still-life of objects with the same hue, or of white objects. Study these objects carefully. Make a small test drawing and work out, by mixing colors, the range you will need to undertake the project. Use your color wheel as the basis for mixing opposites, including warm and cool colors. White can be added for lighter tints. Study the reflected light on the objects with great care, and look for subtle effects. Always test your colors on scrap paper first. Look for the shadows cast by the objects, as these will create the contrasts you need in the work.

This project is a preparation for developing ideas creatively with color. It will help you later to deal with illustration and understand the effects of photography.

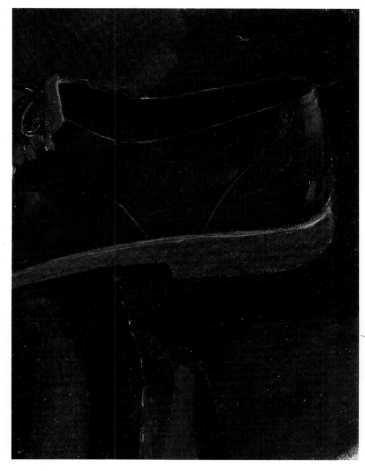

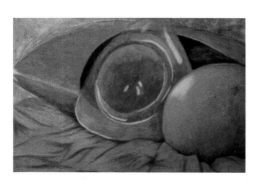

■ **Complex colors** The illustrations on this page have tested the students' ability to mix the right color. Test out your colors first on a separate sheet before applying them to the main illustration. Smaller preparatory color sketches are useful.

Studio techniques: CUT AND PASTE

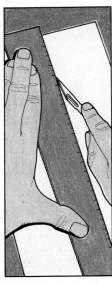

■ Safety Cutting calls for some important safety precautions. Never cut using a plastic instrument as a straight edge, as the knife may cut into it and then into your finger. Always use a steel or steel-edged rule. Hold this securely with your index finger and thumb, holding down both the ruler and the paper you are to cut. The ruler should be positioned so that you are pulling the knife across the paper. Keep the knife well away from your body, moving it from left to right (or vice versa if you are left-handed). Never pull a knife directly toward your stomach. When changing an X-acto knife blade, do not touch the sharp edge, and always push the blade off away from your body.

Besides your drawing skills you will also need technical skills. These can be acquired through a series of elementary exercises. First you will need a sharp X-acto or craft knife. You will need a steel ruler to use as a cutting edge, a plastic ruler, and a right-angled triangle and T-square (for drawing rectangles and dividing spaces equally and accurately). You will also need masking tape, medium and hard pencils, scissors, an eraser, a cutting surface – thick cardboard will do – and a selection of glues. If you choose to use a spray glue, you will also need to make a simple spray booth that will contain the glue during use.

Drawing and accurate cutting

You can now begin a series of cutting and pasting exercises. These will test the accuracy of your measuring, your skill in creating neatly presented images, and your visual powers in linking images.

You now need to learn how to use just the right amount of glue. Too much will spread out beyond the edge of the item that is being glued, making the work sticky and likely to

CUTTING AND PASTING EXERCISE

Draw six uniform squares on a single sheet of paper. Find a black and white newspaper photograph and a color photograph or illustration. Crop the black and white photograph to create a powerful composition that fits one of the six squares. It is best to use an X-acto knife to cut newsprint. Do the same with the color photograph or illustration. Paste them into position.

Next, using a sheet of colored ledger bond paper cut a square and paste this into position. Then, find an image printed on cardboard, such as a cereal packet. Cut out an interesting composition to the same size and paste this in position. The fifth square should be divided into quarters. Using a newsprint image, a color image, the colored paper, and the cardboard, make four separate squares and paste these together in the fifth square. Their edges should fit tightly together to complete the square.

Finally, divide the sixth square into four strips, allowing a thin measured space between each strip. Cut out four strips from newsprint, board, colored paper, and

magazine print. Cut these accurately so they fit within the square, leaving an equal white space between each of the strips.

When you have created six separate images and pasted these in position on your sheet, you can then experiment with making an illustration of your choice using cut and carefully torn paper and images from magazines and newspapers. This illustration should be expressive, fun, but above all cleanly pasted-up.

Take some found type images and see how many different forms of the same letter you can find. Then cut and paste these together to make an interesting layout.

Use a mixture of found type images to create a complex design, allowing the letterforms to dictate the design.

Finally, create a collage background with cut-out letters that spell the word "TECHNIQUES," pasted together into a single picture.

gather dirt. Too little glue and the item will lift and fall off. Practice until you get it right. Always keep your hands clean and free of dirt when using glue.

Planning and drawing as a preparation for pasting are essential. If you are cutting out a square you will need to draw the square in position on the paper to which it is to be attached. You need not use heavy lines, just light indications created with a hard pencil. You now need to cut a shape to fit the space you have drawn. This can then be offered up to its position to fit between the pencil lines.

Do not try to position the entire shape in one go. Offer two corners up to the drawn marks, and when these register allow the cut-out to drop gently into place.

Try doing this with four equal squares placed together to make one larger square. This should soon tell you how accurate your measuring and cutting have been. You can still be creative while you are doing this kind of work. Experiment with combinations of images to produce unusual or contrasting textures, colors, or shapes.

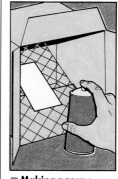

■ **Making a spray booth** Take a large cardboard box and tape the flaps so that it is rigid. Use a knife to cut a large flap in one face, leaving it attached by the bottom edge. Push the flap inward to make a platform inside. Take a piece of chicken wire or similar and fold this so that it fits into the box. This will provide a base on which you can place the paper to be sprayed without it becoming attached to the wire or the box itself.

■ **First exercise**
1 Take a piece of black and white newsprint and cut it into an attractive composition. Paste it carefully into position.
2 The next illustration shows cutting

magazine paper and pasting it into position.
3 This illustration shows a piece of paper cut to size and pasted into position.
4 This collage is made from a mixture of thin card boards cut from

cereal packs. Sharp instruments and strong glues are required.
5 The illustration shown here combines the materials of the previous four exercises.
6 The final exercise

tests ability to cut small strips accurately and to paste them into a precise layout.

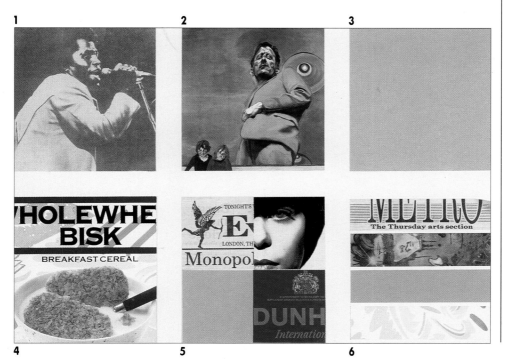

Continued on next page

Torn and collage shapes

Tearing is another form of image-making. With accurate and thoughtful control, you can use torn images to create pictures, producing interesting illustrative effects useful for all kinds of graphic design tasks.

The pasting of images together in this way is known as collage when it involves papers, drawings, and type, and montage when it is a combination of photographic images.

You can combine carefully torn images with those that have been cut with the knife to compose interesting designs. For this you will need a selection of old newspapers and magazines of many different kinds. You may have some idea of the kind of images or pictures you wish to create, although you will come across a lot of the visual information by chance as you leaf through the material.

The student graphic designer will eventually manipulate type and understand the various results that emerge from its use. To prepare for this, an exercise that develops your skills of type recognition can be enjoyed using the newly acquired skills of cutting and pasting. By finding various letterforms in magazines and detaching these either by cutting or tearing, you can reassemble them into interesting designed patterns.

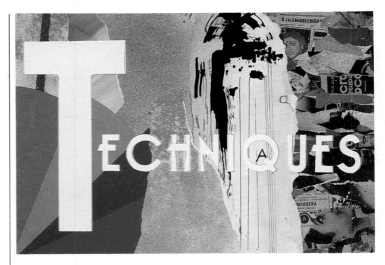

■ **"TECHNIQUES" Collage** The letterforms (above) are carefully cut from existing printed type. The background design is made up of torn and cut found papers which complement the layout and overall design.

■ **Illustrating with collage** is an expressive method of image-making: tearing, cutting and assembling colored images in picture form. However, it does require a large range of source material.

■ **Type and collage** A good preparation for using typography effectively is to cut out as many different styles of type as possible and rearrange these into an experimental design.

— Two types —

■ **After gluing** always place a clean white sheet of paper over the item that is being stuck down, and rub this down firmly using the edge of a ruler or triangle. This helps in two ways. First, you can ensure that the paste-up is firmly in place, and secondly it keeps your hands from smudging your design with any color or inks that they have picked up.

■ **Pictures with letterforms** Here samples of letterforms culled from various publications create a picture which reflects their shapes. The sensitive way these are displayed illustrates an awareness of the individual character-istics of the type forms.

T I P S

■ Always use a sharp knife and a steel edge when cutting.
■ Cut in a direction away from your body — never pull the knife toward yourself.
■ Make a spray booth if you plan to use spray glue.
■ Test out the glue to find the best amount to use.
■ Rub down the paste-up, using a sheet of paper between the image and the ruler or triangle.
■ Always draw lightly the shape you are working within.
■ Different materials need different pasting techniques.

Studio techniques: FOLDING AND SCORING

■ **Scoring** is required to create a straight fold on this board. Use the back of the X-acto knife blade or craft knife and a steel rule to make a light score. Alternatively the end of an X-acto knife handle can be run along the edge of a ruler to make an indentation. Remove the blade first.

1

2

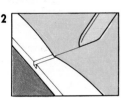

■ **Making a tool** You will need a thick sheet of board (or make a single sheet by laminating two thin boards together). Make two parallel cuts about the thickness of the steel rule apart, but not cut right through the board (**1**). Scoop out the groove with the back of an X-acto knife (**2**). Place the board you wish to fold over the groove. Use the end of the knife holder and a ruler to push a groove into the board (**3**).

There is an art to folding and scoring different grades of board or paper, and its thickness will generally dictate how this is best done. For example, illustration board needs to be scored before folding. To create a clean edge to the external fold, cut the board lightly on the fold and fold inward away from the cut. To do this, with a steel ruler measure up the folds you wish to make, and draw in a line accurately, making sure that the lines are light, square, and in proportion. Keeping the piece of board flat, place the ruler along the drawn line, and allow the blade to cut the surface of the board gently along the line. Repeat this on all the folds, making sure that you always cut to exactly the same depth by controlling the degree of pressure you apply to each cut. Try this out first on a scrap piece of the same board. If you do not cut accurately, the score appears ragged when it is folded.

To fold thinner boards and to create professionally finished folds, you can use another technique, for which you need a simple tool. Take a thicker piece of board and attach it to another piece of the same thickness so that you now have a double thickness of the board. Cut a channel into the board slightly larger than the width of the edge of your steel rule and to a depth of one of the layers of board. Make sure that the channel is absolutely straight and is longer than the fold you intend to make.

Mark up the board you want to fold on the right side, drawing the folds accurately and lightly in pencil. Place the board with the pencil line directly over the channel, with the good side toward you. If the surface is delicate you will need to cover the board with a thin sheet of layout paper to prevent damage when you are scoring. Place a heavy right-angled triangle along the line you have drawn on your board, and, with the rounded

end of your steel ruler, gently stroke repeatedly along the line almost as you would with a knife. The effect of this is to create an indentation, not a cut, in the board along the channel. Remove any protective paper, and fold the board away from you so that the facing surface is on the outside. This will create a neatly folded edge with a slight ridge on the inside of the fold. Most board containers are constructed like this, and with these two techniques, you should be able to make many three-dimensional constructions.

3-DIMENSIONAL LETTERFORMS EXERCISE

Construct a three-dimensional interpretation of the word TECHNIQUES, using a variety of materials and cut letterforms. You will need to plan this out first with working drawings, showing how the letterforms are going to be shaped and which will be three-dimensional. Keep it to a manageable size. Then test your skill further by making this three-dimensional layout into a folding pop-up. (You can find out how this is done by looking at children's pop-up books.)

TIPS

■ Decide which thickness of board requires a cut and which can be scored
■ Make sure that the depth of cut is consistent throughout
■ Fold the board so that the cut or scored edge is on the outside
■ Use a protective sheet when scoring delicate surfaces

1

■ Pop up design in two-dimensional and three-dimensional forms. Work out the mechanics of how the 3-D forms can fold flat.

1 This is the top sheet, scored in the middle allowing the design to unfold by lifting the flap back on itself (below).

2 The design for the word TECHNIQUES is seen unfolded . The pop-up letters NIQ are arranged in such a way as to fold back into the design when the flap is replaced.

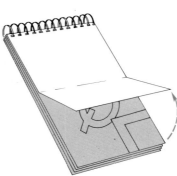

2

■ Gouache tests
Practice mixing gouache before attempting a finished piece of work

1 Mix up the first test to give a flat, opaque cover, with no streaks.

2 Take two color mixes. Paint one on the left and one on the right side of a piece of paper. When these patches are dry, stipple the first color over the second color.

3 Mix up a light color and paint a flat area. While it is still wet, take a darker shade and blend with even brushstrokes.

35

Studio techniques: MEDIA

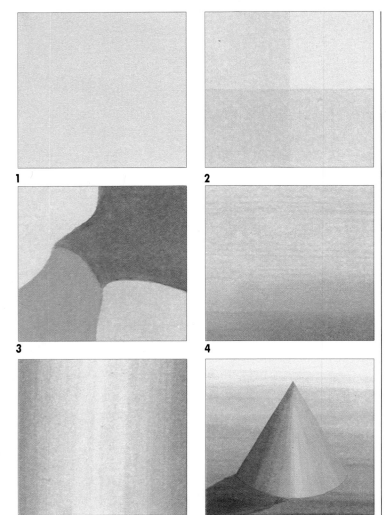

The graphic designer needs to be able to handle different media when working up ideas and visuals.

Designer's gouache is a versatile, water-based paint. Ideally suited to making opaque colors, it can be also used dry and stippled over colors to create tones, or two colors can be blended to gradate into one another. They are especially good for rendering or indicating type on visualized graphics where you need to overlay type on an illustration or photograph. You can also rule straight lines with gouache, either by using a ruling pen, or with a brush and rule.

Gouache comes in tubes, and is normally diluted with the minimum amount of water necessary to achieve a creamy consistency. For mixing you need a jar of water and a pan palette. Soft-haired brushes – the best quality are sables – are used to apply gouache.

MARKERS IN SQUARES EXERCISE

Draw six equal squares on layout paper and use a broad-nibbed marker. (1) Create a flat gray or colored area. Cut it out and mount it on the first square. (2) Next, lay down two different gray tones horizontally, with a sharp edge between the tones. When these are dry, go over half the tones again, this time using the marker vertically, to create two more tones. Cut this out and mount it in the second square. (3) Now divide an area into four different segments and draw in four different flat tones or colors with crisp edges where they meet. This becomes the third square. (4) Create a flat tone, and while this is still fresh quickly work over it in the same direction to change it into a gradated tone. Cut and mount into the fourth square. (5) Now paint a gradated scale of vertical color patches, from dark to light to dark again. Cut and mount this in the fifth square. Finally, draw a three-dimensional cone, showing light and shade, using markers only. Cut and mount.

■ Marker exercises

1 This flat color was achieved using a broad spirit marker applied with quick, horizontal strokes on layout paper. A larger area was colored, which was then cut to size and pasted in position.
2 These tonal overlays were created by making a flat color first. When this was dry, the same marker was applied with vertical strokes over half the area, and when this was dry, a third layer of horizontal strokes was applied.
3 This design of touching colors was produced by drawing up the areas lightly in pencil. These were filled in carefully using different-toned markers.
4 The graduated tone was created by applying a flat color quickly. Before this had dried, the same marker was worked into the tone to produce progressively darker areas.
5 The cylinder effect was made using the techniques of the previous exercise without the initial flat colour.
6 This cone incorporates all of the above techniques.

Ordinary drawing paper is suitable as a surface. If the paper cockles, you are applying too much water.

Professional markers

Markers, both spirit-based and watercolor-based, are available in many sizes and colors. If you use a fine watercolor marker for base lettering or fine line detail and then put spirit-marker colors over the top, you will avoid damaging the line work. Spirit markers tend to dissolve the spirit colors underneath as further overlays are made. Of course, this effect can be created deliberately, too, to blend the edges of colors together, as you would with gouache. In fact, spirit markers are often used for illustrating or coloring artwork, because, if used skillfully, markers can create the impression of a photographic image. Pantone spirit markers have reference numbers which a printer can match to actual printed colors. Thin-nib watercolor markers are good for making thumbnail sketches.

The right choice of paper is the key to successful marker work. Layout paper takes marker pens better than any other surface. It

TOUCHDOWN

■ **Designs made in marker** This illustration illustrates the technical virtuosity of markers.

■ **Illustration and type** This example is based on a dynamic black and white photograph. First a tracing was made of the photo and redrawn on to the layout pad. The tonal contours of the photograph were recreated in permanent markers. The letterforms were then drawn on the illustration with gouache.

T I P S

■ Make sure that your preliminary pencil drawing lines are erased before overlaying the colors with your markers; otherwise not only will they be sealed into the design, but they will be smudged by the watercolor markers.

MIXED MEDIA
EXERCISE

Create a number of experimental illustrations of the same subject, using paper, colored pencils, markers, gouache, overlaid images, photocopies, acetate, etc.

■ **Media tests**

1 In this wax resist test, the image was drawn on the paper with clear wax. The colored ink laid over the top was resisted by the wax.

2 A diffuser was used to spray water-soluble colors to create soft, gradated patterns.

is also ideal for sketching initial designs which can then be taken further by overlaying another sheet and tracing the images. Once your design is complete, you can mount it on a heavier paper or card.

Today's ranges of colored papers are eye-catching. Apart from the rainbow hue of colors available, there are many different textures, printed patterns, and motifs, from a simple matte surface to a soft, silky finish. They can be cut or torn into shapes for collage-effect illustrations.

Colored pencils and chalks

Colored pencils and soft pastels give a more delicate effect than robust markers or gouache. Apart from being popular for illustration work, they are also useful for thumbnail sketches. As with markers, you can overlay colors to create further variations. Pastels can be combined with most media although, like charcoal, Conté, and some soft pencils, they do smudge easily, and will need fixing both while you are working and after the drawing is finished.

Other media

Plastic film (clear acetate) has become an essential design tool for making overlays of color or images and, at its most practical, for overlaying an image, artwork, or photograph with type, such as headings, captions, or legend. Acetate is specially designed to take designer's gouache.

Black and white and color photocopies offer great scope for image making, particularly for enlarging or reducing illustrations and photographs, and of course type, all of which can be manipulated tonally.

The computer is the designer's tool of today and is discussed in more detail on pages 106-9.

■ **Same subject, different media** The designer should be sensitive to the qualities of each medium. Acrylic (top) lends itself to dry brush technique. The impact of the same subject is altered when painted in gouache (above).

3 Rubbings made in pencil or crayon over textured surfaces are a good way of creating an interesting background.

■ **Gouache and collage** make a lively still-life.

■ **Gouache applied in flat colors** with other colors and highlights stippled over the base hues to build up the forms.

4 A dramatic effect is realized by cutting and reassembling an image.

5 Apply markers over masking tape or rubber cement. When these are removed, white paper is left exposed.

6 Black and white photocopies can be tinted with inks or watercolor.

7 Draw a design, then cut a stencil or series of stencils to mask out parts of the image.

8 Spread India ink over dry white gouache. Wash the image to remove the gouache.

9 Use wax crayons or oil pastels as a resist, with inks overlaid.

10 This illustration is made up of watercolour and pencil, combined with cork.

11 A snakeskin effect from gouache overlaid on watercolor.

12 Cloth-like texture from flat color overlaid in white gouache.

T I P S

- Used dry, gouache can be stippled over painted areas.
- Never add too much water to gouache, as this will cockle the paper.
- Buy a set of broad-nibbed grey spirit markers, from light to dark. Add to this a range of fine markers, including black.
- Work on layout paper with blotting paper or layout underneath to absorb bleed.

- Gouache paint can be used over spirit markers for whiting out and highlighting.
- If you use markers with a ruler or triangle, keep the edge of the ruler clean with mineral spirits.
- Masking tape or low tack tape will create a straight edge when working with drawing media.
- The photocopier will give you different tones. You can also photo-copy onto acetate.
- Tracing paper can be used to diffuse images.

13 Photocopy through trace filters and textured translucent materials to manipulate an original image.

14 Copy can be rendered straight onto clear acetate film. Colored plastic films are a quick way of enhancing the images when doing visuals and presentations.

Studio techniques: CAMERA HANDLING

Every designer should be able to take a simple photograph for a number of reasons: to help him or her work out rough ideas, establish proportions, and understand composition, and as a support to drawing.

Few professionals graphic designers become involved in this specialized image-making process. Their role, as yours will be, is to commission or select photographs to solve design problems, rather than producing the finished pictures, which is the job of the professional photographer. However, it is important for the designer to have a basic understanding of how to operate a camera, take a photograph, and create an image with that photograph. Start collecting a library of photographs illustrating as wide a range of styles and approaches as is possible. This is an excellent introduction to the process of art-directing photography.

■ **Visual brief** An accurate illustration in preparation for the studio session will help the photographer to set up, style, and light the subject.

Art direction

Eventually, one of your responsibilities will be to buy in photography. This will mean commissioning photographers and guiding and encouraging them to produce the particular picture you are after. So being thoroughly prepared is mandatory.

Professional photographers often specialize in particular fields or subjects, such as fashion, food, or sport; identifying these individual abilities will be part of your initial research and selection when you are working out your first ideas. It goes without saying that if you are not clear in your own mind what you want, there is every chance that the photographer will be confused too. It is a good idea to write down his brief, perhaps an accurate visual of how the photography is to be set up. This is your starting point. Now you are free to discuss the color and lighting, whether you want the image soft or sharp, or if you are looking for a special effect. The photographer's experience in handling his equipment and his skill and judgment in interpreting your instructions are then brought into play.

Having the confidence to talk about the details of the shoot with the photographer will come much more easily if you learn to take your own pictures. Most design students start off with a 35mm camera and black-and-white film. Once you have experimented with the range of tonal images and exercised your compositional skills, you can then develop your own film and control your results in the darkroom. There are a number of black-and-white films, ranging from slow to fast speed, which have individual advantages. The slow films are more suitable for enlargement, giving a crisp image with a wide range of tones. It is better to use slow films, mounting the camera on a tripod to avoid camera shake and consequent blurring. Using the faster films will give you a grainy image, with the detail breaking up on enlargement. So your choice of film will dictate the results you get. The most popular black-and-white film for general light conditions is a slow speed film, ASA 100-125.

Darkroom effects

Having developed your roll of film, you can now judge whether the exposures are correct by checking the density of the gray tones on

■ **Slow film**, ASA 32 produces a fine-grained image and a good range of tones, and is ideal for big enlargements. A tripod is necessary.

■ **Medium film**, ASA 125 is a fine-grained film that is slightly less sharp than ASA 32. Shots taken with it can be hand-held.

■ **Fast film**, ASA 400 gives a grainy result when enlarged but is ideal for low-light situations.

■ **Very fast film** ASA 100. Image detail breaks up under enlargement, the finished effect is very grainy, with less contrast than slower films.

■ Developing

1 Pour out the developer and check that its temperature is 68°F (20°C). Make sure the room is in complete darkness. Cut off the end of the film.

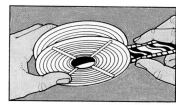

2 If using a stainless steel spool (above) attach the end of the film to the spike or clip at the core and rotate the spool to thread the film into the grooves.

3 Cut the end of the film off the spool, lower the fully loaded spool into the developer tank, and replace the lid; it is now safe to turn on the light.

4 Recheck temperature of the developer, and pour it quickly into the tank. Tap the tank lightly to disperse any air bubbles, and fit the cap that covers the hole in the lid.

5 Start the timer (preset for development time). For 15 seconds in every minute of development, agitate the tank by rocking it backward and forward.

6 At the end of the development time, quickly pour out the developer and pour in a stop bath. Agitate for 30 seconds. Pour out the stop bath and refill the tank with fixer.

7 At the end of the correct time, pour out the fixer. Attach a hose to the cold tap and the other end to the core of the spool. Wash for at least 30 minutes in gently running water.

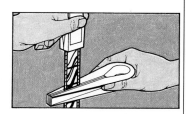

8 Add a few drops of wetting agent before removing the spool. Unreel the film, attach it to a drying clip. Use squeegee tongs to remove excess moisture. Hang up to dry.

your contacts with a magnifying glass. Contacts are made by exposing negatives onto printing paper, resulting in a sheet of images the same size as your negatives. Look for good contrast and any frames that are out of focus. Once you have picked the shots you want from the contact sheets, you are ready to make prints, and the way in which you make that print will have a direct effect on the finished result.

Simply put, a print is made by shining light through a negative onto light-sensitive paper. The more intense the light that strikes the paper, the darker the image, so that, for example, a dark jacket would appear clear on the negative. This would allow a high degree of light to pass through it and hit the paper to form a dark image. After exposure to light, the development and fixing of the image on the paper takes place chemically.

Clearly, this process of exposing the paper to light gives scope for a great deal of experimentation. You can "vignette" the photo, which gives it a soft gradated edge, following any shape. This is achieved by cutting the shape you want out of black illustration board and holding this between

■ Darkroom techniques

You can make your own negatives: by drawing with ink on clear acetate and exposing the light through this onto photographic paper you will achieve a print like the one shown above left. You can also use the exposed film at the end of the roll: scratch at the emulsion with a sharp instrument and you can form a graphic image such as you see above right.

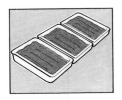

■ **Contact strip** Dust off the negatives with anti-static. Place them emulsion side down on to a clear sheet of glass. Place another sheet over this to make a sandwich. Adjust the light from the enlarger to shine on all the negatives. Place the bromide paper (grade 2 is usual) emulsion side up, underneath the negatives, and expose them to the light for five seconds, increasing or decreasing the light according to the effect you want.

Processing a print
1 Check that the trays of developer, stop bath, and fixer are in the right order, and that the developer is at 68°F (20°C). Reduce the lighting and make the exposure.

2 Slide the paper, emulsion side down, into the tray of developer, and push it down with developer tongs so that it is completely submerged.

3 Turn the paper over so that the emulsion side is facing up and you can see the image developing.

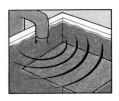

4 Rock the tray gently to agitate the solution and so ensure even development. Develop for 90 seconds.

5 Use tongs to lift the paper out of the developer tray and allow the excess solution to drip off. Put it in the stop bath, taking care to keep the tongs out of the solution. Rock the tray gently as before.

6 After 10 seconds, lift the print out, drain, and transfer it to the fixer tray for 10–20 minutes, agitating the solution at intervals. After a minute or two, the print can be examined.

7 Wash the print in running water. For washing time, see what the paper manufacturer recommends: resin-coated papers need four minutes, paper-based papers need about 15 minutes.

9 Paper-based prints should be dried in a flatbed print dryer (above). Glossy prints are glazed by placing them face down on the metal plate. Most professionals use glossy paper unglazed.

the negative and the light-sensitive paper as the light is shone through the negative. With careful positioning and some trial and error, you will achieve exciting results.

You can also reduce the amount of light that strikes some areas of the paper by blocking out part of it with your hand or a piece of board before it strikes the paper. If you then allow the image through, you will be able to control the shading or brightness of it by hand.

Light-sensitive paper will give you an image of a type, without a negative. For example, to make a photogram you put an object on the paper and expose it to the light. Where the light strikes, the paper will turn dark; where the object blocked the light, the paper remains white. Hand-made negatives can be formed by drawing on acetate, and positives by working directly on the surface of the printing paper.

Black-and-white photographs may be hand tinted or colored. And inks applied to a print or washed over in tints will create special illustrative effects, allowing you to transform a rather ordinary photograph into an arresting or unusual one.

Cropping

One important aspect of photography is knowing how many pictures can be extracted from a single shot. Cut out two L-shaped pieces of board and use these as a device for finding other compositions in the same photo. Lay the L-shapes on top of one of your prints in the form of an adjustable rectangle. Move them around the photograph looking for new arrangements. It is surprising how many different shots can be found in a single photograph. Designers often have to make the best of photographs that are not always suitable at first sight, but skilled cropping can transform a mediocre image into a stunning visual.

Color photography

The majority of color pictures used in design work are color transparencies, ranging in size from 35mm up to 10×8in. Transparencies, in contrast to color prints made from color negative film, give you a consistent colored picture and are processed either by the manufacturer of the film or, better still, by a professional laboratory. Color prints, on the other hand, are often of indifferent quality although 85 per cent of all amateur photographers ask for them.

With the advances in color photocopying, transparencies can now be enlarged to whatever size you want to paste up in position in your design.

PHOTOGRAPHIC
EXERCISE

Choose a theme such as wealthy, poor, old, modern, dangerous, political, angry, etc. Seek out a location where you are likely to discover suitable images that reflect your subject choice. Take a number of pictures, trying to make the most of the light and compositional arrangements, and to emphasize the point you are trying to make. Make a contact strip of the pictures you have taken, select one or two images for enlargement, and make a print of the subject. Make a number of smaller compositional photographs cropped from the main image.

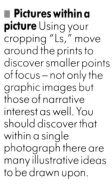

■ **Pictures within a picture** Using your cropping "Ls," move around the prints to discover smaller points of focus – not only the graphic images but those of narrative interest as well. You should discover that within a single photograph there are many illustrative ideas to be drawn upon.

Exploring ideas: SOURCE MATERIAL

A major aspect of the graphic designer's job is to make the most of a given assignment, however bland and devoid of inspiration it may appear to be initially. This is where the exploratory approach illustrated in this book, together with sound visual research, will give you the skills and the vision to tackle such a commission with confidence. How do you view your subject? What ideas spring to mind? These are the key questions the designer must be able to answer.

By this stage of your work you should be eager to investigate the visual world that you are training for. Your library is a launching pad for this activity, and as you explore the information it holds and search out fresh material, remember that artists have always been influenced by ideas and styles from other sources and other centuries. Use this information wisely to generate new ways of looking at things; but don't fall into the trap of conscious copying of the work of others. Instead, look for the way an image has been interpreted: is it in a linear form, in solid shapes, textural, or collage? Has color been applied to change the form? How does the composition affect the subject matter, and what mood is conveyed? Is it aggressive, lyrical, harmonious? And what is the shape of the image itself?

Now is the moment to start your sketchbooks and scrapbooks. Carry a sketchbook at all times to jot down ideas; the scrapbooks will contain the images you have cut out from magazines. Everything that pleases you should be kept.

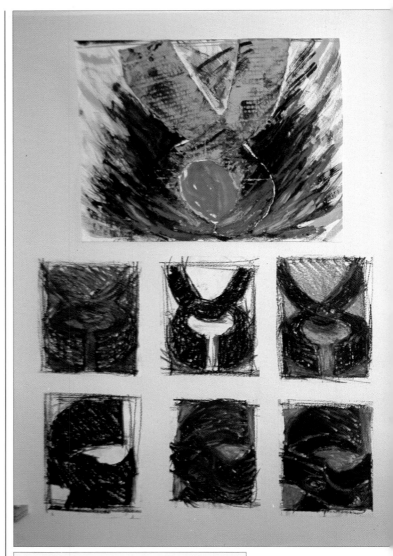

OBJECT EXERCISE

Take a simple object and investigate the nature of the object through a number of exploratory studies. See how many ways you can interpret it or moods you can create through it. Take one idea and develop this to a higher level.

■ **Worksheets** Start by investigating the different shapes an object makes; explore the tonal qualities of color and image; or try to express the nature of the object and its function. In the case of these pliers, the student had managed to convey the aggressive qualities of the tool.

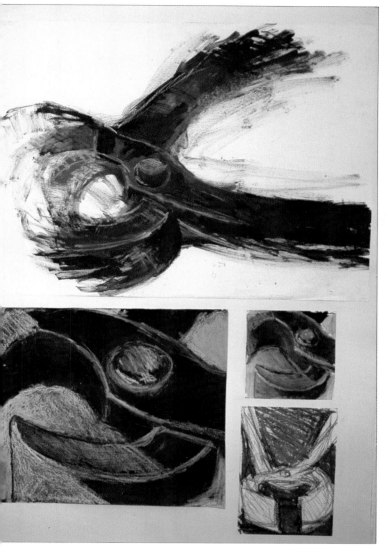

■ Choosing a layout is a key factor in design work, so understanding how to manipulate elements within a space is vital. The illustrations of a portion of a can (below) represent layouts in which a single object is the theme. Think about the use of color, the different styles of drawing, and the shape that can be created within the space.

■ Taking detail This graphic interpretation of a section of an electrical plug uses abstraction to its fullest potential. The designer has made good use of the shapes to create a stylized design.

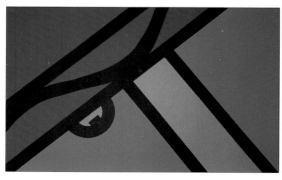

T I P S

■ Use the local library to research the works of 20th-century artists and designers, as well as graphic design techniques.

■ See how many visual ideas can evolve from a single composition.

■ Keep a sketchbook for exploring ideas, and start assembling a scrapbook of images you like.

Exploring ideas: EXPERIMENTING WITH MEDIA

The techniques you apply to your graphic work will influence the way the image looks. If you take a single motif or design and interpret it in a number of different ways, you begin to appreciate how you can effect subtle changes simply by how you use color or media. For example, taking colored papers and cutting out shapes to suggest a visual idea will look radically different from the same image drawn in markers. The paper version will appear mechanical in form while the marker design will keep its feeling of a drawing. The same image, in relief on a piece of board or raised using a resin, will give a three-dimensional effect subtly using light and shade to express the form.

The inventive ways you can approach the same design or illustration are limited only by your own imagination. For instance, bleach can be used on dry water-based ink to create interesting effects. Methods of resist are always worth investigating; you can use wax, colored crayons, and even gouache paint. First, paint the areas you wish to remain white in white gouache on the surface of a piece of board. When this is dry, go over the entire drawn and painted area with black Indian ink. When this has dried, hold the board under a gently running tap and wipe away the gouache as it dissolves. This will leave an image projecting out of the black inked surface. To create gray tones or textures, apply the white thinly or in a stippled pattern. This simple technique will give a convincing rendering of old drawings and woodcuts.

■ **Flat color** Simple areas of flat color or cut-out paper shapes can suggest familiar objects, structures, buildings, and locations. Take an everyday object; without imposing any detail, see how many different designs you can create from it.

■ **Gouache resist** By simply tracing an image from a photograph, such as in the case of this gouache resist of an elephant, you can recreate an image in black and white or color, on white or colored papers.

■ **Stipple and rub-downs** Controlled and careful stippling will result in powerful illustrative images. The same tonal effects can also be achieved with rub-down textures, some of which can be seen in this interior drawing.

■ **Bleach and ink** To create the design above, the artist first painted a flat shape on the paper in water-soluble ink. When this was dry, he drew into the ink with bleach, using a number of different-sized brushes.

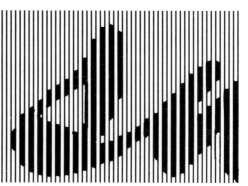

■ **Line work** Technical pens are excellent for rendering tight line drawings and simple illustrations in line where printed definition is poor.

INITIALS
EXERCISE

Take your own initials and form these into a simple design with block letterforms (keep it bold and simple). Explore the use of different materials and different techniques, and see how many ways you can interpret the letterform combination.

■ **Finding an image**
Take some traditional type images. Select the letters that represent your initials and see how many different shapes can be created using the letterforms. You may wish to follow the found letter images faithfully or stylize them as this student did with his initials SSS.

■ Embossing
1 Draw your design in soft pencil on tracing paper Turn this over and transfer it onto thick board.

4 This leaves you with your design in reverse cut into the board.

5 Lay thick drawing paper over the mold you have made. Take the handle of a brush and gently push in the paper along the grooves, taking care not to press too hard.

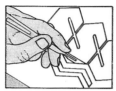

2 Use a sharp knife to cut along the lines, but not through the board.

3 Lift out the cut board, leaving a groove along the line of the design.

■ Alternative images
Create some alternative visuals based on the design you have created. Do not change the design in any way, only the technique or method used.

Airbrush This method of illustrating utilizes graphic skills for cutting and masking, and then requires carefully controlled spraying.

T I P S

■ Create different versions of the same image but do not change the drawing.
■ An accurate trace will help maintain consistency.
■ Try cut-out media; rub-down materials; transfer systems; resist techniques; tone techniques; stipple; cross-hatch; swelled line and different line techniques; ink and bleach; airbrush.
■ Try embossing your image, or using relief, as in thermography.

49

Exploring ideas: FINDING THE RIGHT IMAGE

All designs must be relevant to the job to which they are related, and whether this relevance is direct or implied, the appropriate image which suits the subject has to be found. How do you initiate this process?

First you need to look at the subject itself. What is the message here? Look at a number of suitable illustrations to see whether these suggest a possible design to you – one that will allow you freedom to experiment with different approaches. Remember what you have learned about the various techniques of graphic image-making, from drawn images to photography. For instance, for a zoo poster there are many aspects to be explored, not simply the animals themselves. What about the sounds they make; the different textures of their coats; the colors; and the environments created for them? There are the people who look after them and the behavior that all the animals display – including the human ones.

You will not always be able to follow your scheme through to a satisfactory conclusion simply on your own technical expertise, however. Few graphic designers can. You do not have to produce all the images. Some images, perhaps a photograph, or an illustration in a suitable medium, will be beyond your scope. For roughs or presentation material it may be enough to borrow illustrative material to make your design points – you will, of course, have to seek out permission from the creator of the work. Once your idea has been approved by your client, you will then either buy a suitable photograph from a picture agency or commission the work from an illustrator or photographer.

POSTER DESIGN EXERCISE

Pick a subject that you can have access to, such as a zoo, a museum, the local library, your neighborhood restaurant, etc. Work on location. Find a photograph or illustration that best conveys the feeling you are trying to express about your chosen subject. Do a number of rough visuals to test the layout until you are completely satisfied with the idea and the way it is developing. Give your poster a title: "Zoo," "Library," "Museum," or "Restaurant." Use existing type images. Design the finished poster to a size that displays these elements well.

■ **Points of interest** A first impression can be developed into a graphic idea. Here, in a poster for the Science Museum, London, the student has picked up the idea of a hand, signifying humanity, shown as an x-ray, signifying science.

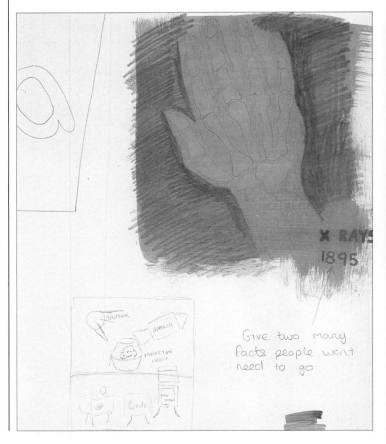

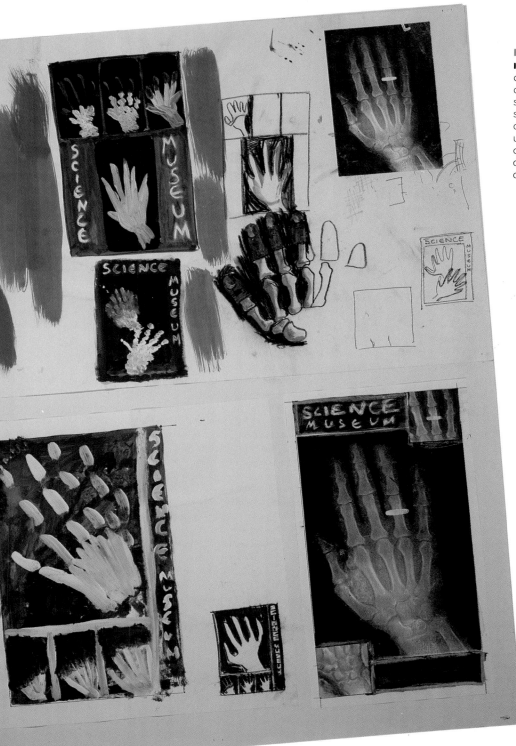

■ **Exploring a visual idea** The x-ray idea is obviously worth developing. The next stage is to work out some different approaches. Yellow is used to emphasize two other scientific discoveries: artificial light and photography.

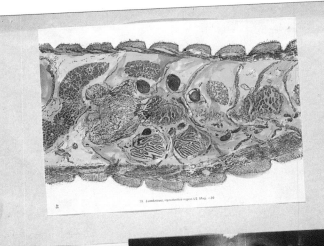

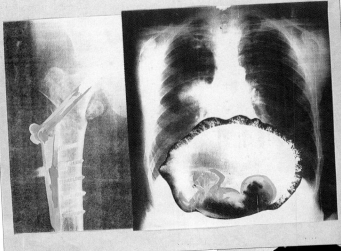

■ Other directions
Although the x-ray hand suggests a good image, the designer's purpose is to search out the approach that works most effectively, perhaps by looking at other parts of the body with other scientific techniques. Here the designer has explored the images given by heat-sensitive photography instead.

■ Which works best?
Once an idea appears to work effectively, the designer then firmly eliminates all the other possibilities. The hand x-ray provides the strongest graphic image so the next stage is to develop the idea to a presentation visual.

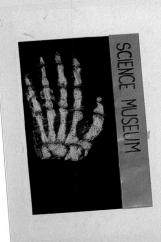

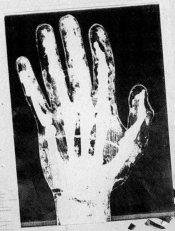

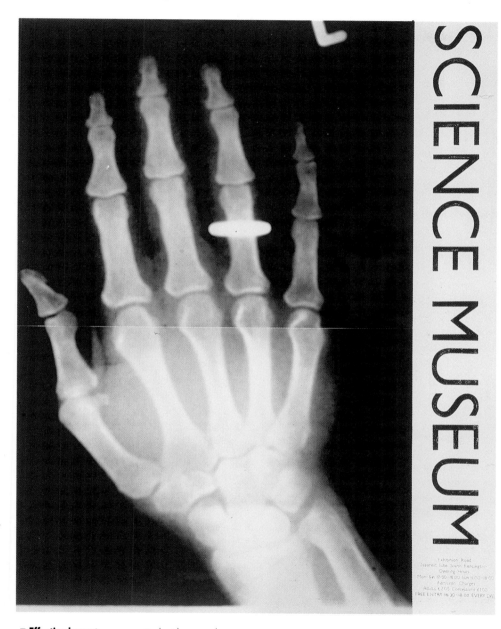

SCIENCE MUSEUM

■ **Further ideas** may still spring from the visual conclusions you have discovered. The visual here explores an idea of using projected lights.

T I P S

▼

■ Pick just one subject, but investigate a number of ideas based on the subject.
■ Look for simple, direct images that will make unusual visuals.
■ If you cannot draw, find a drawing (or a photograph) that works for you.

■ **Effective layout** does not have to involve complex shapes, forms and techniques; often the simpler the technique, the better the effect. For this layout the student has used an actual x-ray rather than attempting to visualize a complex image.

Introducing type: BASIC PRINCIPLES

■ Type through history
1 Example of early Greek alphabet, from which our alphabet is derived.

2 Inscription taken from the Arch of Titus, Rome, c. A.D. 72. Copies of incised serif letters.

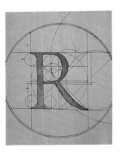

3 This illustration shows how some classical letterforms were geometrically constructed. The letter is engineered out of a series of circles and straight lines.

The essence of good graphic design is communicating via the written word, often combined with a drawing or photographs. Over the centuries the art of displaying the written word has evolved into a highly sophisticated area of graphic design. Words, and the images they create, come in many styles. Each letter of a word can be viewed as an illustration, and it is the designer's job to choose the right letterforms to communicate the message.

Letterforms

As far back as ancient Egypt, ideas have been communicated in visual form. The Egyptians used drawn pictures and symbols arranged in lines. Our letterforms have their origins in ancient Greece, where written symbols were also displayed in lines to convey messages and create words. Indeed, our word "alphabet" is Greek, relating to the first two letters, alpha and beta. The graphic designer uses letterforms in two ways: to communicate through words, and as images themselves that have forms and shapes that can be manipulated. If you think of the letterforms you choose as designs in their own right, you will be well prepared to create interesting layouts with typography.

Serif letterforms have their origins in the past, when letters were chiseled into stone slabs, but it was difficult to ensure that the edges of the letters were cut square. So the carver developed a technique of finely overcutting a cross line to finish off most of the letters. This created a style that has continued to this day. The thickness of lines used in modern typography to make up letterforms also has its origin in history. Early rendered letterforms were hand drawn using a quill. The quill's flat nib gave different thicknesses of line, and this feature was retained for its natural beauty and styling.

Roman letters were based on perfect circles and balanced linear forms. The round letterforms such as o, c, p, b, etc. needed to be slightly larger because optically they appear smaller when grouped into a word with the other letter shapes. If you draw a line connecting up the base of the letters in a printed word, you should be able to detect the overlap of the round letters. Letters such as l, t, m, h sit on the line, whereas the round letters dip slightly, breaking the line, but creating a visual balance.

There are three groups of letterforms: serif, slab serif, and sans serif. The family of serif typefaces includes those with very thin serifs and those with wedge-like serifs or even block serifs. The traditionalist would claim that the only true serif is one based on a perfect curve from a true circle and finishing in a point; all others fall into the category of slab serifs.

The third category of letterform is the sans serif. These have no serifs, and are used today for many different types of printed text. Sans serif letters, however, are rarely used for large amounts of text, as it is now generally accepted that the flow of the serifs leads the eye more easily across the printed page.

Upper and lower case

You will need to familiarize yourself with some special terms which describe the components of type. For example, a set of type all of the same design is known as a "font." The letterforms were stored in trays with the small letters in the trays below and the capital letters in the trays above. Consequently the small letters became known as "lower case letters" and the capitals as "upper case letters." Letterforms were then gathered together to make words in a "stick." Once a line was created it was then transferred into a "galley." Once the whole galley

Find a large typeface. Draw in lines to indicate the cap height and the x-height. Select three letters: one capital, one with an ascender, and one with a descender. Draw them in pen, achieving a visual balance with the spacing.

Using all the terms covered in the preceding sections, draw a series of letters to illustrate them. Render these letters neatly together using a black fine liner.

ABcdefgh
ABcdefgh

■ **Roman** describes both serif and sans serif upright letterforms.

ABC abcde

■ **Serif** letterforms are those whose main

strokes finish with a cross stroke.

ABCabcde

■ **Sans serif** Some more modern typefaces have evolved without serifs.

These are known as sans serif typefaces.

■ **Traditional typesetting**

1 Traditionally the typesetter worked from a number of cases containing individual pieces of type. The upper cases contained capitals and the lower cases contained the small letters.

CAP HEIGHT

Abg

ASCENDER

X–HEIGHT

DESCENDER

■ **Sample letterforms**
Use typesheets and tracing paper to render the letters you have chosen accurately and in proportion to one another. Draw them first with a sharp pencil, then ink them in using either a technical pen and black ink or a permanent fine line marker.

2 Each letter was placed in the "composing stick," and the words and lines were spaced using pieces of lead.

Sans Serif   Serif

UPPER CASE (CAPS) lower case

Roman   *Italic*

Light   Medium   **Bold**

Expanded   **Condensed**

Script   Outline   Slab Serif

DROP SHADOW (SHADED)

■ **Rendering typefaces**
See how many different typefaces you can find. How many different styles are there to be seen? Taking the words shown here (left), render them in an appropriate typeface.

3 When the type had been set it was placed in a galley, where a hand print could be made by inking the type.

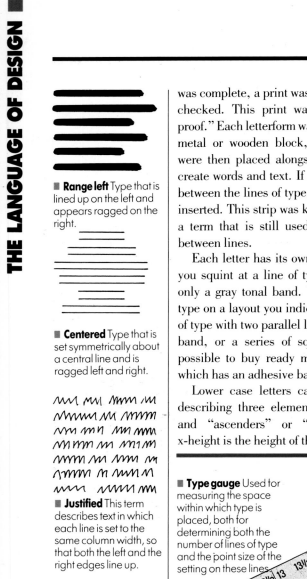

■ Range left Type that is lined up on the left and appears ragged on the right.

■ Centered Type that is set symmetrically about a central line and is ragged left and right.

■ Justified This term describes text in which each line is set to the same column width, so that both the left and the right edges line up.

■ Type rule Used for measuring type, in points and pica em units. One pica equals 12 points.

was complete, a print was taken off this to be checked. This print was called a "galley proof." Each letterform was cut out of a single metal or wooden block, and these blocks were then placed alongside one another to create words and text. If space was required between the lines of type, a strip of lead was inserted. This strip was known as "leading," a term that is still used to indicate space between lines.

Each letter has its own characteristics. If you squint at a line of type you will detect only a gray tonal band. When you indicate type on a layout you indicate this tonal mass of type with two parallel lines, or a solid gray band, or a series of squiggles. It is also possible to buy ready made-up body type, which has an adhesive backing.

Lower case letters can be specified by describing three elements: the "x"-height, and "ascenders" or "descenders." The x-height is the height of the body of the lower case letter. An ascender is a feature of the letterform that rises above the body of that letter, as in b, d, h, etc. A descender is the part that drops below the body of that letter, and consequently the line of the type, such as in the letters p, y and g. Capital letters, upper case, are specified by "cap height," and these larger letters are normally the same height as the ascender of the lower case letter.

Type size

Type is traditionally measured in "point" sizes. You will probably see type sheets with a large variety of alphabets of different sizes, with a number printed alongside, followed by the letters pt, the abbreviation of point. There are approximately 72 points in one inch (25mm), so the point system measures the space the type will occupy. If you draw a series of horizontal lines, 12 points apart with a type gauge, your 12 point letterforms

■ Type gauge Used for measuring the space within which type is placed, both for determining both the number of lines of type and the point size of the setting on these lines.

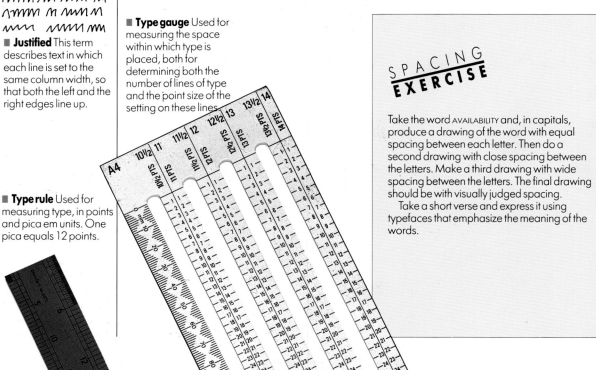

will fit between these two lines, with sufficient space for the ascenders and descenders to sit within that space. However, if you wish to print 9pt type in a 9pt space, you may find that the lines appear cramped. To create more space you will set this 9pt type in, say a 12pt space, effectively leaving 3pts between each line of lettering. You will often see type with varying degrees of space between the lines. These spaces are created by "leading" the type.

When indicating type on a rough, use the type gauge to rule the lines in, or use one of the techniques for indicating type. Remember, if you are indicating a bold type, the lines you use will be heavier than those that indicate a light typeface. Type is normally organized into columns, the width of which can be measured in pica-ems. One pica-em represents 12 points, so 72 points equals 6 pica-ems, or roughly one inch (25mm).

Having decided on the width of your columns, think about the shape you want your text to be, because, naturally, lines of words are not all the same length. There are a number of options: the lettering can all be "centered," which means it will make a balanced shape around the vertical center of the column. It can also be "ranged" to the left or to the right of the column, leaving a "ragged" edge on one side. It can also be "justified." This means that the text is typeset to create straight vertical lines on the left-hand edge of the column and the right-hand edge of the column. To achieve this, it is necessary on some lines to break or hyphenate words or alter the "word spacing" so that an even column of text is formed.

Copy fitting

When you are faced with a large amount of text to be fitted into the design, you need to work out how much space this text will occupy. This technique is known as "copy-

■ **Rub-downs** Sheets of type are available for rubbing down onto your work.

1 Draw a faint line and place the bottom of your rub-down letter on this.

2 Use a ballpoint or stylus to rub the letter gently into position.

3 Then lift the sheet of letters away so that you can examine your work.

AVAILABILITY
AVAILABILITY
A V A I L A B I L I T Y
AVAILABILITY

■ **Letter spacing** Try this exercise to practice rendering and spacing and to investigate the different spacing required for different typefaces. You should also try out different instruments for rendering.

■ **Rendering** The more practice you give to rendering typefaces the better your skills will become. Do not overlook the correct spelling of the words. Clients will be highly irritated by such errors as in this passage about granite.

The block of **GRANITE** which was an obstacle in the pathway of the *weak* became a **STEPPNIG - STONE** in the pathway of the **STRONG**

T I P S

■ If you are indicating type for a visual, you should use a type gauge. Mark off the number of lines you want at the desired point size. This gives you the depth of your copy, and between these lines you can fit your chosen type size.

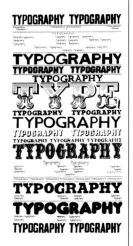

■ **Type as image** Type is not just a means of conveying words – it also creates a visual image. Use it to create an interesting design. Color can also be subtly introduced to emphasize a point.

fitting." You know how much space you have for the design and how much space you want to allow for the copy. You also know the width of this copy, since you have already roughed out the columns. Next, you need to establish what size the type should be set to occupy the space and accommodate all the text. You find this out by counting how many "characters" (or letters), word spaces, and punctuation marks your text has. A simple way to do this is to count the characters or words in an average line and then multiply this by the number of lines in the text. You have now established approximately how many characters or words there are in the entire text.

With the style of the type selected, you must then choose the appropriate point size which allows the right number of characters to fit your space. This can be done in two ways. The easiest is by means of the casting-off table normally found at the back of the printed typesheet. Take the width of your column and read off the table how many characters can be fitted into each line at different point sizes. For example, a 10pt typeface may allow you to fit 50 characters per line. If your total text had 1,000 characters, then you will need to be able to fit 20 lines of 10pt text into the space available. If this does not fit, you can increase or decrease the point size or put in leading.

The other way to fit copy is to count the number of characters in a printed example of the size and style of type you wish to use and compare this against the length of your own text. There are some shortcuts to working out the numbers of words in a given text. In the English language, the average word has approximately 5 characters. A 1,000-word text therefore has about 5,000 characters. Add to this 1 character per word for word spacing, and the total to allow for is 6,000 characters for every 1,000 words.

Spacing headings and letters

Large-sized type is an important feature of much design work, and it therefore should be rendered with accuracy and precision to replicate exactly the finished type. It is a good idea to practice tracing letterforms from typesheets. Select a large point size, and draw in the x-height and cap height lightly with pencil on tracing paper or thin layout paper. Draw fine lines with a liner pen, and render the type shapes as accurately as possible. You can transfer this onto another surface by first drawing carefully around the letters in pencil, then making a carbon sheet by applying a soft pencil to the back of the paper on which the letters are drawn. Rub the carbon with your finger so that it makes a solid patch. Turn the sheet over onto the fresh surface you want to work on, and re-draw the lines of the letters, pressing through to the paper below. The outline of the letters should be lightly transferred.

The spacing between letters also needs consideration. If you space each letter equally, there will be a visual imbalance in the word you have formed. Compare four letters in a row: two vertical letters next to each other equally spaced, followed by two round letters, also with the same spacing. The two verticals will appear cramped, but the two round letters look too far apart. So the spacing between the letters has to be calculated visually. There is no formula for this, other than to consider the amount of space between each letter, judging by eye each letterform with its neighbor. You will see that two vertical letters need more space between them than two round ones.

JUSTIFIED

Designing for print is one of the most stimulating challenges any designer can face. However, there are several fundamental problems to be taken into consideration – the two most important being the varying width of the actual alphabetic characters and the difficulties of word spacing. Without some understanding of both problems, the end product may well fail the twin tests of attractiveness and legibility in some cases.

■ Specifying type
Heading: 18pt News Gothic, Ranged left.
Body copy: 9/10pt News Gothic, justified × 12 pica ems.

This is the way to specify typesetting. It should then appear like the piece shown above.

JUSTIFIED

RANGE LEFT

RANGE RIGHT

CENTRED

■ Visualizing type layouts
You can render every word in the text in the style in which it is to be set. This is both unnecessary and extremely time consuming. Find a way that expresses body copy economically.

■ Type layout
Type can be made to look formal or informal, light or bold – in fact in any style that satisfies the visual requirement, as in these examples.

Franklin-Antiqua Regular

Franklin-Antiqua
Regular

■ **Your initials**
Experiment with the
letterforms that make up
your initials to create
different effects.

Type and technology

Today's typesetting machinery is computerized. No longer do individual characters
have to be grouped in a wooden frame.
Type can be arranged on a computer screen
simply by pressing keys. This is not to say
that all the technical know-how of typesetting, from point sizes to galleys, can be
ignored; type terminology remains the same.
same, and while column widths and cap
heights are specified in millimetres, as well
as points, most machinery accepts both
systems of measurements.

There is no disputing that modern typesetting processes and desk-top computers give
the designer enormous flexibility with typographic imagery. Typestyles can be made to fit
your ideas, rather than adapting your needs
to what is available with traditional setting.
Typefaces can be condensed and expanded,
more spacing can be placed between letters
and words, type can be wrapped around
illustrations, and made to perform all kinds of
acrobatics, without having to cut between
individual letters – and all within a matter of
minutes. But like much modern technology,
the computer has its limitations, and it is the
designer's job to find the best way to achieve
the results he or she is aiming for. Some
computerized typefaces carry the type name
followed by a qualification, such as Roman,
Book, *Italic*, **Bold**, Expanded, Condensed,
Outline, Light, Medium, **Heavy**, and **Black**.
These terms describe either the characteristics of the letter or a word such as Book
suggests its application. Roman means upright type and Black, sometimes confused
with Gothic, is extra heavy.

■ **Newsletter** Type can
be used to express a
mood. Try rendering the
headings for a
newsletter in a style that
communicates their
meaning.

PLANTIN
Plantin was first designed by Christopher Plantin (1514 -89).
Plantin monotype series 110 was cut in 1913. It was designed to incorporate inkspread into a typeface.
Plantin is mostly used for display work and newspapers.
Plantin is now available in *Italic* as well as ROMAN.

■ Expressive type
Experiment with letters to create illustrations out of words. Be sure that your message is legible.

■ Type posters These poster designs exploit the shapes of the letters to emphasize the style of the typeface. You can also see how letters can be changed pictorially by tonal variations. Researching the type history will help you understand the type's historical context.

T I P S

■ Letterforms should be viewed individually as illustrations.
■ Remember that type communicates a visual message just as a drawing does.
■ Serif text is easier to read in a large amount of type.
■ Take advantage of the quick methods of indicating type on your layout.
■ Spaces between the lines of type can be added to fill a design area.
■ When spacing a line of large type, look at the amount of space between the letters.
■ Fine liner pens are ideal for rendering type.
■ Trace your type using type sheets.

Preparing for print: TWO-COLOR ARTWORK

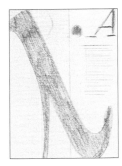

Mechanical print methods demand visual instructions from the designer for the printer to follow. If your design is in a single color, the printer will make only one printing plate, block or screen. This is simply loaded into the print machine or placed on the screen in accordance with your instructions, and the finished image can be printed in any one color. The plate is an etched metal sheet that carries the image. It is made from your artwork and will reproduce the work exactly as you have drawn it. A block follows a similar principle. In screen-printing (see page 65) the image is carried on a screen, and the areas that are not to be printed are blocked out.

Artwork is the last stage in the design process before it is handed over to the repro house and the printer. Clearly, if more than one color is involved, another process separates these colors out at artwork stage. Photographs and illustrations to be repro-duced in full color, require special treat-ment. Here we are creating areas of flat

color which can be artworked by you.

Each color is printed from a separate plate. To demonstrate this, let's create a piece of artwork that is separated. Take a piece of stiff line-board — a rigid surface that will carry an overlay, plus some technical pens to draw up the shapes on your artwork, plastic rules and set squares, hard pencils, and plastic trace overlay for the second color.

The process of sticking the design ele-ments down on artwork is known as paste-up. First, tape your line-board down on to your work surface. Draw up the elements of your finished visual on to the line-board lightly and squarely in pencil and within the design area. Text will be set photographically, ready for gluing to the appropriate color layer. Include registration marks for location of overlays. These lines lie outside the design area and must align on every layer of artwork or the result will be colors out of register.

The most prominent color will be on the first layer of the artwork, the base board.

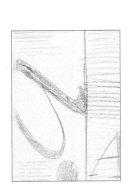

A R T W O R K
EXERCISE

Create a design in two colors based on your initials. Develop it to an accurate visual and then to artwork.

■ **Thumbnails** Show your versatility by using your own initials inventively to create a number of alternative thumbnail sketches.

■ **Visual** Take the idea that expresses the most satisfying approach (right). Render this accurately, separating out which area is going to be printed in which color. Make sure that your visual is presented so that the design is shown in the colors in which it will appear.

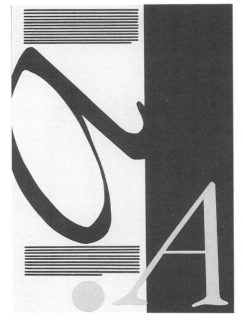

Draw the area in outline with black ink and technical pen, using set squares and rulers, and French curves or ellipses if necessary. Now fill in the areas with brush and ink, or black gouache. Overlap the boundaries of the design area by about 3mm (⅛in). This is known as "bleed"; it will be trimmed off when the work is cut out and ensures that the color runs right to the edge of the printed area.

You may wonder why you are producing a color using black. This makes it easy for you to produce the work and easier for the printer to photograph in the plate-making process. Remember the color is placed in the printing machine so at this stage it is not affected by your artwork. All printed artwork is produced in black so any marks or lines which you do not want reproduced must be properly erased or obliterated before the artwork is handed over to the printer.

The second color

The plastic trace overlay, the matte side facing up, is the work surface for the second color. Tape it to the base artwork along the top. Draw the registration marks on your overlay. Now tape together firmly. Indicate the areas of second color on the overlay, as you did with the first color.

Next, the printer needs a color guide for each artwork layer or a Pantone color number. The printer also needs to know what size to print your artwork. You can make your artwork larger than the print size to make it easier for you to draw in fine detail, giving the printer an accurate measurement for him to reduce the work. If it is to be printed the same size as your artwork you need only an instruction to print "s/s".

T I P S

■ Think of each color as a separate image.
■ Work in black, using artwork pens and ink. You will need a large soft brush for painting in the solid areas of color.
■ Masking tape can be placed in a strip under the plastic ruler and triangle to ensure that the ink does not smudge along the edge of the plastic.
■ Clear, accurate cropping and registration marks are vital.
■ Ink will be slow to dry on the plastic overlay. There is a powder available from art supply stores which speeds up drying when sprinkled over wet ink.
■ Make sure your artwork is fixed to your drawing board so that it can be drawn up accurately.

■ **Artwork** Produce accurate artwork for your design, drawn in black on illustration board. Place registration marks on each corner outside the image area. Fill in areas that are to be printed in solid color in solid black. For the second color, place the overlay onto the base artwork and draw in the registration marks. Draw your design, and fill in solid color areas in solid black and specify colors.

PRINT BASE BOARD, PANTONE 541

PRINT OVERLAY, PANTONE 277

Preparing for print: PRINTED IMAGES

The purpose of most graphic design work is to build an initial idea through to the point where it is printed. But the print process can, in fact, influence the way that concept is carried out. Therefore, it is important to experiment with simple printing to see just what effects can be created. Naturally, there are restrictions with each kind. Take lino-block printing, for example. You might use this process to develop the idea in terms of shapes and textures. First you plan your design on paper. Once you have decided on the image you wish to print, you are ready to cut your design into the surface of the lino, taking into account the size and number of colors you want. It is wise to start with a single-color design; printing on a colored paper will give you a second color. Having finalized the drawing, make a careful tracing of this. The next step is to turn the tracing over and go over the lines carefully again on the actual surface of the lino. The design is then cut out of the surface of the lino with a number of different sizes and shapes of chisel, leaving the areas to be printed in relief. After the lino has been inked, lino and paper are then pressed together in a sand-wich to transfer the ink to the paper. Although lino cuts are normally printed with ink, you can try oil or acrylic paints, or oil pastels, blended with white spirit or turps.

Once you have created your first linoleum print you may want to experiment with over-printing in different colors. Line up your paper carefully to be sure that the subsequent colors register where you want them. There are many other exciting and inventive ways to make prints. Try cut and collaged corrugated cards, wire mesh, any woven material, or cork. Not only will you have the fun of creating images in a different way, but you will also find it useful when creating textured surfaces or backgrounds.

LINOLEUMCUT EXERCISE

Take a simple message or illustration and work out the areas that will be solid and those that can be textured. Keep the design bold to allow as much print surface as possible. Trace your image onto lino with soft pencil. Chisel out the areas that are not to be printed, leaving the image itself in relief. Background colors can be prepared on the paper first, and allowed to dry. Using a small roller, lay a surface of colored ink over the cut. Place the lino down firmly on your sheet of paper and press down evenly to print. Try this again, inking parts of the lino progressively.

Linoleum cut Linoleum is an easy and inexpensive way of creating a bold and expressive image. Use a range of inks and papers to get different effects.

■ **Screenprint**
1 Because silkscreen inks are opaque, you can create a background color by using an empty screen filled with ink – in this case blue. Alternatively, you may wish to use colored papers.

2 Your design is now transferred onto the screen with the areas not to be printed blocked out. Choose your color, in this case white, and print over your first color.

3 An outline effect is produced in a third color, printed on top of the first two. The inks must be dry before applying each separate color.

Screen printing

This process can accommodate designs ranging from the simple to the complex. Screen printing involves inking a fine mesh placed over paper. A squeegee is pulled across the surface of the screen, forcing the ink through the mesh onto the paper. Where the mesh has been blocked, the ink is prevented from penetrating, resulting in patches of un-inked paper.

The images can be placed on the mesh using three methods. The first and simplest is to block out certain areas of the mesh with a blocking agent, available from craft suppliers. Or you could use a special film which is cut by hand according to your desired design. This is then fixed to the surface of the screen. Finally, in the photographic method, images are transferred onto a light-sensitive film, which reacts by fixing the image to the screen, and allows the surplus to be washed away by ordinary water.

Using more than one screen will result in a multi-colored print, and with their opaque qualities, colors can be layered over one another to produce bold, graphic images which, at their best, can be complex and sophisticated fine art prints.

T I P S

■ Experimenting with a number of printing techniques is often helpful in making design decisions.
■ Don't forget that most graphics are ultimately printed.

■ Keep your print experiments simple to begin with.
■ Print backgrounds first if other colors are to be overlaid.

Chapter Two: PRINCIPLES AND TECHNIQUES

So far in this book we have explored various media used for the creation of images. These provide a link between vision and the way that it can be expressed. Now further possibilities open up.

This next chapter builds on your visual knowledge and describes how you can begin to explore ideas. But you should think about the assignment before you begin to put down any images on paper.

You will need to draw on all the knowledge you have already gained. You may want to apply free expression or a tightly controlled form – either realistic, abstract, or decorative. You may need to do historical research to

■ **Right** A poster inspired by research at the Victoria and Albert Museum.

"pretty poorly"

Every year, hundreds of parrots die due to Man moving them from their natural habitat. We're trying to save this beautiful bird from extinction. Support us by telling your friends.
THE WORLD WILDLIFE FUND

■ **Left** An effective visual executed in marker pen.

determine the image. Does color play an important part in the idea? Or perhaps black and white can give you a sufficient choice to make your statement.

How you compose your subject is vital, and you will need to try various different ways before you move on to another image. By experimenting in the processes required to complete the projects shown, you will learn more about the way in which ideas develop.

You will discover how you systematically select and reject various graphic elements. Every decision you make will need to be justified to ensure that the route you take clearly follows the instructions. This part of the book establishes the methods you will employ to generate ideas and develop them into a successful conclusion.

Free image-making: SOURCES OF IDEAS

However technically skilled the graphic designer, he or she must still be able to devise inventive solutions to set problems. And every designer is constantly looking for, and experimenting with, new ways of expressing these visual ideas. It is not enough merely to arrange graphic elements within a design framework. New concepts, new approaches have to be sought out and wrestled with to give life and vitality to design in the future.

One vital way of exploring the vast possibilities of image-making is to develop an appreciation of fine art techniques and movements, music, architecture and literature. For instance, if you were designing a poster for a concert of classical music, would it be sufficient to know the sounds made by the music, the mood it creates, and its physical and emotional aspects? Surely it would be more telling actually to listen to the sound and *feel* the effect it has on you. You would then respond personally to the task, and the result would be your own interpretation. The sounds would give you ideas on shape, form, color, texture, and rhythm. In the same way, your response to graphic design should now go beyond simple technical competence, to explore a region of original thinking.

Linking mood and image

Look at images by photographers and painters and try to understand their intentions. Imagine the personality behind the work and the emotions displayed in it. Investigate the moods created by photographs. Go through the archives of mass circulation, popular magazines, looking at images and how they are used. Look at the way advertisers manipulate imagery to target specific audiences.

Try a simple exercise. Take three very different pieces of music. Listen to the first piece. On a sheet of paper, with your drawing

VISUAL EXPERIMENTS PROJECT

Select an object from the following: a pair of shoes, a selection of candies, a vase of flowers. Research the following categories, principally in terms of the visual arts but bearing in mind that these categories also cover literature, music, architecture, etc. Expressionist, Romantic, Constructivist.

Your job is to consider your object in all three ways. Don't consider the chosen object purely in terms of the style of the art movements but according to their particularly emotional qualities. Remember that scale, layout, color, and media will all affect your interpretations. You should end up with at least three finished pieces (one for each) and a great deal of back-up experimental work to demonstrate your analysis of the research and many different approaches.

■ **Expressionist image**
This example of a student's finished piece has brought together a range of influences. The student has understood the simplification of line, the use of strong, vivid color, as seen in Rouault's work, and the emotional force in expressing a visual idea.

■ Constructivist images
The art of the Russian Revolution has had an enormous impact on 20th-century graphic design. Here the images show the typical use of angular shapes and mechanized forms common in art from this period.

■ Romantic images
The Romantic Movement offers more of a challenge to students than the previous two. By understanding the main exponents of this movement, notably Delacroix, students can learn ways of manipulating imagery so that the artist's interpretation is imposed upon the viewer. These images project a carefully chosen Romantic approach.

and painting media alongside, try to express in color and movement a vision of what you hear. Carry out this exercise with the other two pieces of music. Pin the work up and evaluate the images you have created. Assess the differences and consider how you can improve or develop the pieces of work.

This work will require color experiment to make the right visual link between what you feel and how you express it. For instance, it is not sufficient to settle just for a red image. You have to describe precisely the nature of the red you are experiencing. Is it a warm red or cool? Is it passionate or fierce? The degree of subtlety implied in the work will be the key to its success.

You can set yourself all kinds of similar projects. How would you express your own personality visually? Would you need to start with a portrait and move on to more abstract forms? Once you understand yourself, you can then use the same techniques to understand the thinking of others. This preparation, although it may appear obscure, is closely linked to the creation of corporate images (see Chapter 3). You can see by studying the logos of various companies how appropriate they are for the company, yet how abstracted they can be from their source. Letterforms, too, can be developed and crafted into shapes that are distinctive and individual, but the designer can achieve

TIPS

■ Set up a situation that stimulates an emotional response, and explore this visually.
■ Free yourself from conventional approaches.
■ Use any medium; do not feel restricted.

■ **Constructivist worksheet** This demonstrates how a Constructivist image can be created from the simplest object – in this case a chocolate bar. The sketches below look not only at the position of the elements of the bar but also at its color quality.

■ **Expressionist and Romantic approaches** The images (right) explore the different possibilities of the two approaches. The moods are quite different: one dark, heavy, and oppressive tones, the other light and whimsical.

successful expressions of a company's inner characteristics only when he has developed his own confidence and vision.

Basic lessons

By pursuing image-making with careful thought and by observing the characteristics of the subject you are studying, you will learn how to investigate with depth and sensitivity. This will give you another dimension to your approach to design which goes beyond technical competence.

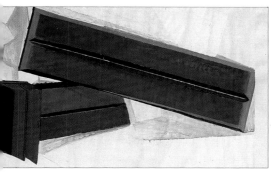

■ **Revised Constructivist image** The work has now been revised but the Constructivist influence is still apparent. The student's objective approach to drawing depats from strict Constructivist practice.

■ **Working large** This image demonstrates the necessity to allow yourself space for full and free expression. The student here has worked on two large sheets of paper.

Type and layout: PRINCIPLES IN PRACTICE

■ **Study the forms** Do not look at the image created by a piece of type as just a letter. Use it as a designed form, and experiment with it, as these examples show.

As we have seen (pages 54-61), type is made up of designed images: each letterform or number is like an individual piece of sculpture. Even the punctuation has been designed for its visual and illustrative potential. Don't feel restricted by conventional sizes of type; think of letterforms as images that can be used on any scale that fits within the design space.

Having accepted this premise, you can create all manner of exploratory visuals. Look through typesheets at the style and design of quotation marks, for example. Imagine these enlarged by a factor of 100 (or enlarge them on a photocopier). Look at the shape again. Enjoy the shape within a space, the "negative" shape. Imagine that you actually have a quote. Relate this to a quotation mark. See how many alternative visuals you can create.

You can reverse the quote out of the black shape by indicating the type in white with a fine brush and gouache on the black surface. Or, alternatively, you can produce your quotation mark in white on a black background and place the black type inside that. Why not run the type around the edge of the symbol, or use the type to form the shape of the quotation mark itself? When you have exhausted these possibilities, move on to the parentheses, colons, hyphens, and exclamation marks. You will find that a great many visuals can be created with the question mark.

Although the same exercises can be done with numerals, it is more exciting and visually stimulating to take the same numerals from different typefaces and mix them together. As an exercise, try filling a sheet of paper with these different designs created in varying sizes. Study each of the numbers for their form, and choose those that please you the most. Then see what images you can create with them.

■ **Experiment** Use letters and numerals to make pictures and patterns. Here, many different variations on the letter A and the numbers 1, 2, and 3 have been used.

Type in proportion

Let's now turn our attention to the layout of type images for everyday applications. There will be occasions where you will use different sizes of type together in your layout. Your client may even specify the type priorities by identifying the information that needs special emphasis. For instance, if there is a sale at your local store, it is likely that the word "Sale" and the discounted prices will take visual priority over all other printed matter. Magazines, books, and newspapers also highlight the importance of certain pieces of text or headings. The headings will

TYPE AND LAYOUT
PROJECT

Choose one of the following topics: a telephone directory cover, a typographic annual cover, a restaurant menu. Create a design using the images from selected typesheets. Do not invent your own. By enlarging or reducing, create a layout that explores your chosen type images. You may also use color. Produce thumbnails and a full-sized, carefully produced visual.

■ **Ideas sheets** The student has begun the project by trying out different forms, different typefaces, and different approaches to laying out the type. Because color will be important in the design, it is included even at this early stage. Many different ideas have been tried – even though some will not be at all suitable.

Continued on next page

be given greater significance than the text; sub-headings will probably lie somewhere between text and heading weight.

Try to think of the words you are arranging in separate categories, perhaps going through the text with different colored highlighters to code the copy and help you organize your design. Remember, your design should stand out, not only for its quality of layout but also for its suitability for the job.

Type in color

How is type used in color, and how does this enhance the message? For example, would you express the word "cold" in reds or yellows unless you deliberately wished to confuse the reader? The design you are creating will represent a product, service, or piece of information, and you will be looking for connections between this and the colors you select. The only way to discover how color and type interact is by exploring many possibilities: each letterform can be designed to be printed in a color of its own; background colors can be used with white letterforms; colored letterforms can be placed onto colored backgrounds; images can be cut out to form the shape of letters; and textures or surfaces can add another dimension to letterforms.

Try cutting some words from colored paper, then mix them around to see what images emerge. If you follow through the idea of type, its punctuation, and its numerals as being sculpted design images, you will soon learn to appreciate their individual features.

By exploring type, you will learn how to manipulate these forms within a shape as objects of aesthetic value, and this familiarity will enhance every aspect of your typographic work.

■ **Choosing a design direction** Create a selection of ideas for you or your client to choose from. Two different approaches are shown here.

■ **Making a visual** This visual was created by drawing the letters on a layout sheet and coloring in the background. The white letters were painted in gouache.

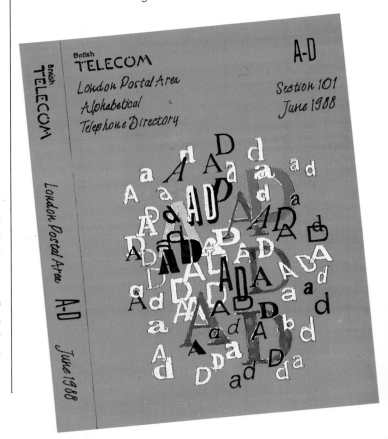

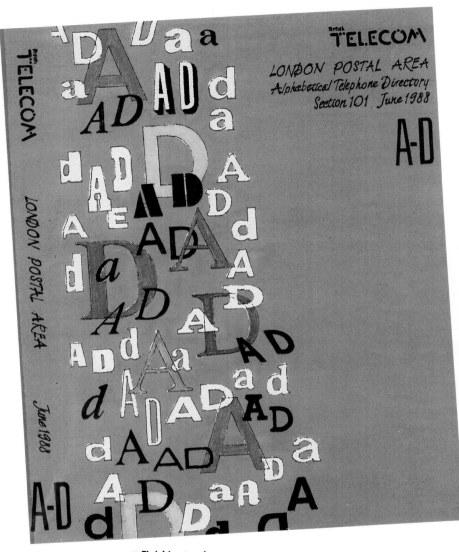

TYPE AND LAYOUT

■ **Finishing touches**
The client may request refinements on seeing the visual. In this case, the student decided to improve the design by showing the letterforms flowing and falling across the entire design area.

■ **Continuity in layout and design** For each telephone directory (below) the letterforms and color were changed. The design remained consistent, the color coding making each volume easy to recognize.

75

The grid is a drawn structure like a scaffolding that underpins the text in books, magazines, and many other designs (see pages 134-135). To use a grid you must first design it. This need not be complicated if you think of it as columns running vertically down the page and arranged at geometric intervals. Columns can vary in width and number on the page, but they must remain consistent within the grid.

■ The grid This type of structure underpins most book and magazine layouts, giving the pages formality and continuity.

First you need to draw the design area to scale, leaving a small margin around the inside of the design area. Divide the space into equal segments. Allow space between these segments so that the columns of text do not touch. This grid can then be used to carry the formal text, while headings, sub-headings and design devices can be arranged around the visual effect of the text. The grid should help you to be imaginative and not require you to follow it rigidly.

Now that you can appreciate how type can be explored for its own image, the next step is the creation of words. A new dimension in the use of type, it is also an opportunity to have fun with words. Remember from earlier sections the terms bold, expanded, light, italic, and so on? These express the different ways in which an individual type style can be presented. Words are more than a representation of a typeface; they can convey a message in addition to the actual mean-

POSTER PROJECT

As part of their eating publicity, the Health Education Authority is running an "eat breakfast" campaign. This is aimed at young people, from schoolchildren who are preparing their own breakfasts to students away from home and cooking for themselves for the first time. Design a full-color wallchart/poster as part of this campaign, using suitable copy. The wallchart must be strong and eye-catching, and will be used in schools and colleges, youth clubs, etc. where teenagers get together. The finished visual should show hand-rendered display typography, and body text indicated with parallel lines or another similar technique. All type must be accurately cast off (copy-fitted).

You will need to create a grid that will carry the columns of copy. This grid should be chosen from one of the following:

Two-column grid

Six-column grid

Five-column grid

This page The pages of this book are set on either a five- or four-column grid. This page shows the underlying five-column grid.

■ Simple four column layout The poster (right) has a four-column grid. The columns of body copy are located on the grid, while the headings break out of it to give the poster more visual interest. Once an under-structure has been created, it simplifies the process of arranging the graphic elements.

■ Complex use of grid By overlaying and interlinking two grids, you can use the vertical structure of both grids to align different elements. In this poster the student has used two grids to create a vertical structure which can be developed in many different ways. The type has been rendered horizontally, ranged with the edge of the grid, and some headings have been set vertically to use this vertical structure.

E A T

B R E A K F A S T

DID YOU WAKE UP TO BREAKFAST...?

DID YOU KNOW...

GETTING ORGANISED

IF YOU CAN'T FACE FOOD FIRST THING...

PACK A PORTABLE BREAKFAST...

CHECKLIST

MAKING A GOOD START...

BREAKFAST SANDWICHES...

LIGHTER IDEAS

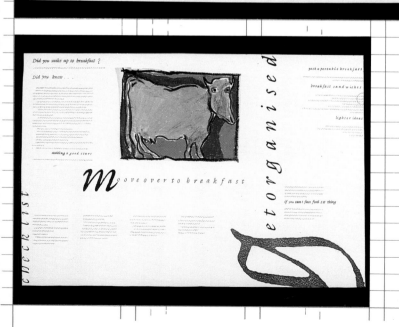

Did you wake up to breakfast ?

Did you know . . .

check list

making a good start

m oveover to breakfast

Getorganised

pack a portable breakfast

breakfast sandwiches

lighter ideas

if you can't face food 1st thing

TIPS

■ Take text, heading and subheading and work out their different proportions within a design space.

■ Try out different typefaces using unexpected combinations. Do not opt for the obvious.

■ Look at the way propaganda and advertising use words visually to communicate.

■ See how color can be used to create mood and tone.

ing of the word itself. For instance, doesn't "granite" imply that the word should be set in a bold, black, weighty type? However, if you set out to confuse the reader, you could use a delicate letterform to reverse this idea. Part of the fun of designing with type comes from imposing your own interpretation on the way the type is presented. As you become more experienced, you will learn just how powerful this effect can be. Study material ranging from 1930s propaganda posters to current advertising. Analyze the message alone, then look at how the type presents this information. Is there any ambiguity between the message itself and what you see?

■ **Ideas** The first ideas were to present the Gujarati carrot salad recipe in a manner that suggested a container or bowl. The typographical mixing of the ingredients in a container gave the project visual interest— important since the assignment insisted on no illustrations. The colors of the salad were to play a vital role.

DISPLAY TYPE
PROJECT

Here are two short passages from *Alice Through The Looking-Glass* and a recipe for Gujarati carrot salad. Select one. Your job is to present one of these in a visually exciting way. There are no limitations on size, format, or color, but the problem must be solved typographically. No illustration, except for possibly a background texture or devices to lead the eye. The format could be a poster, a book, a folded leaflet, a three-dimensional object, etc. A few points to remember:
■ Type does not have to be black.
■ Type can be bold, italic, expanded, condensed, etc.
■ Type does not have to be horizontal.
■ Letter spacing, word spacing, and leading are just as important as choosing the right typefaces.
■ Typefaces have a history—this can help your selection.

1 " 'I should see the garden far better,' said Alice to herself, 'if I could get to the top of that hill: and here's a path that leads straight to it— at least, no, it doesn't do that' (after going a few yards along the path, and turning several sharp corners), 'but I suppose it will at last. But how curiously it twists: It's more like a

corkscrew than a path: Well, this turn goes to the hill. I suppose—no, it doesn't: This goes straight back to the house. Well then, I'll have to try it the other way.' "

2 "It would have been all the better, as it seemed to Alice, if only she had got someone else to dress her, she was so dreadfully untidy. 'Every single thing's crooked.' Alice thought to herself, 'and she's all over pins: May I put your shawl a little more straight for you?' she added aloud. 'I don't know what's the matter with it!' the Queen said, in a melancholy voice. 'It's out of temper, I think. I've pinned it here, and I've pinned it there, but there's no pleasing it!' "

3 Gujarati Carrot Salad (Gujar ka salad)

¾lb carrots, trimmed, peeled, and grated coarsely
¼ teaspoon salt
2 tablespoons vegetable oil
1 tablespoon whole black mustard seeds
2 teaspoons lemon juice

Method
In a bowl, toss the grated carrots with the salt. Heat the oil in a very small pan over a medium flame. When very hot, put in the mustard seeds. As soon as the mustard seeds begin to pop (this takes just a few seconds), pour the contents of the pan—oil and seeds—over the carrots. Add the lemon juice, toss, and serve.

■ **3-D model** In this case a working model was created, to prove its feasibility to the designer and client.

■ **"Alice" type layouts** The student has used two methods to provide an individual design. Words have been either rendered as capitals or increased in size for emphasis. Their meanings have been used as shapes in the layout.

■ **Using shapes** The finished design shown here combines inventive use of color and type which turns the idea of a bowl into an attractive and useful wall chart. It can be displayed as an object and also shows the instructions for mixing the salad clearly laid out. This solution shows that creating three-dimensional graphic objects from a typographic brief is possible.

■ **Introducing fun into type** Another design concept develops the 3-D idea. This puzzle (right) carries all the information required to create the Gujarati salad. The fun element of this design requires the cook to uncover the mystery of the salad by organizing the puzzle in the right order. The two colors reflect those of the dish, whereas different type was used on each individual panel to go with the words used in the recipe.

I SHOULD see the GARDEN far better said Alice to herself 'if i could G E T to the T O P of that H I L L : and here's a P A T H that leads STRAIGHT to **it** at least ,no, it doesn't do that—' (after going a few yards A L O N G the Path and T U R N I N G several SHARP C O R N E R S 'but i suppose it will at last.But how curiously it T W I S T S ' it's more like a C O R K S C R E W than a

Path ' Well, this turn goes to the HILL, I suppose no it doesn't !

Type and layout: ILLUSTRATIVE TYPOGRAPHY

Type becomes much more exciting when integrated with other graphic elements including shape, texture, and illustrative forms. As we have already seen (pages 54-61), letterforms can be cut out and spaced to follow the contours of shapes within the design, and texture can be added to them for different degrees of emphasis: the surfaces of the letters might simulate materials, from fabric to concrete, or special papers can be used. Single letterforms can be colored, or torn from magazines and newspapers.

■ **Curved forms**
Take a strip of letters. Cut carefully between the characters but not right through to the baseline. Stick this in position around an accurately drawn curved line.

Letters and words can be spaced irregularly, perhaps to follow a curve, by setting or rendering the letters first, cutting them out as a strip, and then cutting between the individual letters with an X-acto knife, leaving the strip intact along its base. A photocopier will produce distorted or diffused images: lay tracing paper or other types of transparent material between the image and the photocopier's plate.

In a process known as frottage, letters can also be traced with wax crayons or oil pastels. In fact, you can transfer an image from any printed magazine or newsprint to another surface. Apply mineral spirits with a brush to the image you wish to transfer, lay this face down on the artwork, and with a solid roller, gently apply pressure to the back of the image, releasing a light facsimile of the image – in reverse, of course.

INTEGRATED TYPE
P R O J E C T

Design and construct a three-dimensional information pack for the World Wildlife Fund. Through the design and the typography, convey creatively the problems facing the environment – land, sea, and air – and our wildlife. The text, written to the design, will be simulated. Exploit different media, fabrics, and papers, together with the illustrative techniques. Make thumbnail sketches, then create a full-sized mock-up of the pack.

■ **The idea** The image below shows a made-up dummy expressing the design idea. Tiny slivers of masking tape attach the photocopied type and illustration images to the pack, allowing the possibility of changing elements as the mock-up evolves.

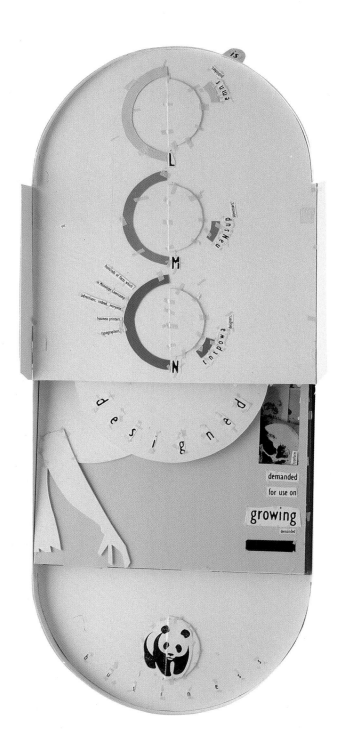

■ **The model** Opening the model (left) exposes the contents – a series of cut-out shapes based on typographic images. Color is used only minimally, so that it does not detract from the message of the typographic image or the cut-out shapes.

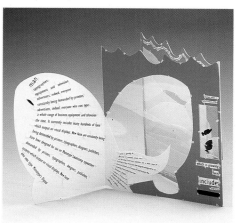

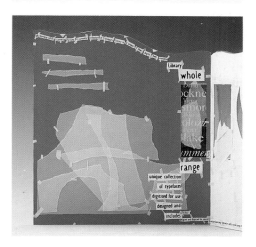

■ **Some of the contents** Individual leaflets inside the pack are also used to provide information creatively. One leaflet is itself a cut-out shape, with type added to give texture and illustration. Another simulates icebergs with torn tracing paper and has a typographic treatment which echoes their shape.

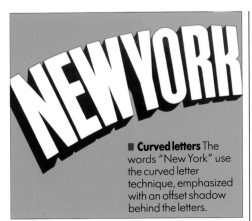

■ Curved letters The words "New York" use the curved letter technique, emphasized with an offset shadow behind the letters.

■ Tyger 1 Concrete Poem by Bob Cobbing, 1971. Studying the way in which type has been used in art helps develop creative typography.

Shadowed letters

By drawing letters and re-tracing them, slightly out of their original position, it is easy to create subtle or dynamic shadow images. These can be printed as the merest hint of tonal color, or produced in bold multi-colored stripes. Letters often become illustrations in themselves, simulating glass or chrome or outlined in color or texture.

■ The Tree A poem by Valerian Valerianovich, 1963. The words have been formed to illustrate the idea visually. Find other ways in which this has been done.

Basic lessons

By exploring the shapes created within the words, or arranging type in a form that complements the ideas expressed in the design, you will successfully integrate illustrative elements to produce bold, lively typographic statements.

ROCK CONCERT
TICKET
PROJECT

The ticket will advertise the venue and the artiste or band. Use their lyrics as a possible background to the design. The typography should be appropriate and add an extra dimension by telling people something about the performers and their style.

■ **Pop concert ticket** For this project (facing page and left) the student has used photocopied typographic and illustrative images. A subtle confusion is deliberately implied, which is added to by the colors. The overall effect is a blend of gothic mystery and modern "arty" imagery, appropriate to the subject.

T I P S

■ Letterforms can be cut or stripped to create shapes and follow contours.
■ Textures or tints can be applied to the letterforms.
■ Don't ignore historical developments in illustrative typography.

Type and layout: ADVANCED COLOR TECHNIQUES

■ Same layout, different colors Here, a number of illustrations of the same set of objects have been produced. In each the position of the colors, or the actual colors, have been changed. A different meaning emerges in the work when different colors are used.

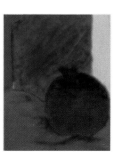

With color, you have the means to transform each or all of the elements within a design. And then by taking those same colors and rearranging them within the design area, you can change the entire mood or emphasis of the work. Many graphic design jobs, however, allow only limited use of color, perhaps just single or two-color options, so also being able to make the most of minimal color is a useful skill to acquire.

Single color is not quite so restricting as it sounds: it does, of course, include all the tints from that color. A dark blue, say, will give you a range of blues, from the subtlest hint to the darkest hue. To demonstrate this range you will need the right tools or paints: it is only with the best quality markers, for example, that you will get the variety of tints

of one color that you need for your visuals.

The balance of the colors – how much of one particular color is applied – will also affect the way the design works. Passionate or moody? It depends on which red you choose and how much of it is used. Color does more than simply suit the subject matter; it can evoke mood; it can shout or whisper your message; it can be youthful or serene; it adds a sense of time and period.

For this exercise, find a simple picture such as a photograph of a face, and reproduce it in background and foreground color only. When you have exhausted the possibilities of single and two-color designs, move on to a still-life in flat single colors. Use the same shapes to create different layouts. Produce as many versions of this as you can,

PROJECT

Create a poster and include a colorful array of objects from the exhibition. These can be symbolic shapes or splashes of color. Demonstrate your color awareness through a choice of different designs, making full use of four colors, and developing your preferred choice through to the final design.

■ Roughs in color
Here, different approaches to the same project use different ranges of colors as well as images. Vary the colors you use, and you will get different effects.

taking trouble to imbue some with a feeling of dynamism; make others quiet and passive. You will discover how carefully applied color, working on many levels, can become the most important element of a layout.

Basic lessons

By starting off exploring a single color and progressing to two and more colors, you will be able to chart the changes and the effects these variations have on the design. Trying out these color combinations is done most efficiently by computer graphic systems, where you can call up instantly any color available on the computer program.

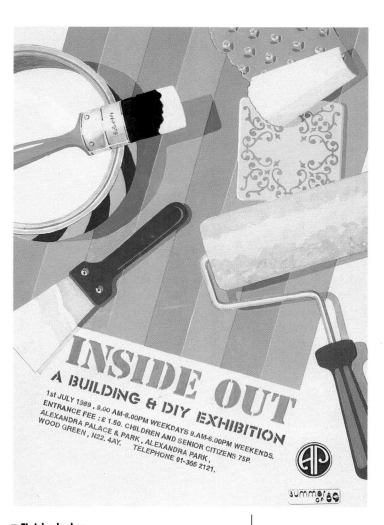

■ Finished color rough The final visual selects color arrangements from the previous pieces. The over-prominent blue has been dropped and the colors given more equal balance to allow the type to appear stronger.

■ Different layouts can change the effect Even once the design idea has emerged, variations in both layout and color will change the effectiveness of the design. These visuals represent the choices available.

T I P S

■ Experiment with switching areas of color around.
■ Quality markers will give you an extensive range of tints for visualizing.

Research techniques: DESIGN IN CONTEXT

In the same way that you will be polishing your graphic techniques, so you must nurture your skills in research. However clear in your mind those initial ideas appear to be, you are unlikely to put your hand on the references you need the moment you walk into your local library. You will probably have to become familiar with its index system first, establish contact with a helpful librarian, and set aside enough time to carry out your research thoughtfully and thoroughly.

Plan the work carefully. Will your time and energy be adequate to cope with rushing from one location to another collecting reference material? Project research time should be planned and budgeted for in the same way that you would cost out an actual job. A good quality hardback notebook is essential for note-taking, references, and quick sketches to record visual ideas. Drawings should always be accompanied by the thoughts that inspired them – they are useful memory-joggers days, and even months, later.

The 20th century has seen major developments in the history of art and design. In fact, the German Bauhaus has probably shaped more modern graphic design than any other single movement. Understanding the philosophy of the Bauhaus and its workshops makes it easier to appreciate the influence and inspiration for much design.

For every image you put down on paper, there is bound to be a previous historical source. Even your own drawing skills will have been shaped by your teachers' interests, the visual bombardment you experience every moment of the day, the chair you are sitting on, and the magazine that lies open in front of you. They should all be grist to the designer's mill.

Fashions and technology have changed our style of life for ever; strange cultures have

ART FAIR PROJECT

Research a period of art history that exploits graphic images, and develop a design entitled "The International Art Fair," reflecting your chosen period. Design a poster and catalogue that work together. Develop your own forms, either graphic or typographic, which are original and follow the historical theme.

■ **First thoughts** The student's ideas were developed from the Constructivist art of the Russian Revolution. This first thumbnail uses a graphic idea from this period and applies it to the name of Stalin.

■ **Testing the style**
Constructivist imagery is developed in this test piece. It uses color and typography in a style much influenced by El Lissitzky and his followers and creates an image which can be developed in further work.

ABCDEFGHIJKLM?
MNOPQRSTUVWWW!
XYZÞÆ[]()€$ 12345 +
67890 ÷

■ Creating a typeface
The student has now developed the images into a full upper case alphabet, which will help in making decisions on the design of the final poster.

■ **Influences** The poster below also shows the Constructivist influences of Joost Schmidt and El Lissitzky, the typographic leaders who also influenced the later design of the Bauhaus.

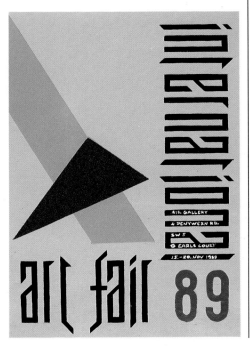

■ Creating a poster
Two poster designs (above) were now produced each displaying changes in color and geometric forms. The final poster (right), developed from this experimentation and was also used as the catalogue cover.

■ **El Lissitzky** A collection of poems by Mayakouski, designed for *The Voice* by El Lissitzky in 1923.

■ **De Stijl** An influential magazine published in Holland by Theo van Doesburg in 1917. Design of this period was highly influential in the modernist movement across all the arts.

■ **At the museum** The task here is to gather as much information and ideas as possible, as notes, sketches, or photographs. This student has selected the historical fashion section at the Victoria and Albert Museum, London.

helped to shape new design movements. For instance, the highly decorative forms of 1960s graphics were inspired by Indian music and philosophy. But how do these stimuli involve the graphic designer? By researching your project as conscientiously as you can, and taking the best from classic as well as contemporary sources, without slavishly copying tired ideas, you will give your work a freshness and originality. It will have something to say.

Market research

The graphic designer's concern goes beyond creating the winning image. The most strik-ing piece of contemporary art may be as indecipherable as a badly written note. Your job is to communicate with your audience clearly and efficiently without ambiguity. This means that the design must be precisely targeted, and it must not over- or underesti-mate its market. To ensure this, market research techniques are now highly sophisti-cated. You can be sure that extensive re-search precedes the launch of almost every new product. Armed with a marketing pro-file, the designer is able to aim his campaign with calculated accuracy. However small the graphic design job, it should still be sub-jected to the same scrutiny: Who is the

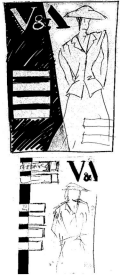

MUSEUM
PROJECT

Select a museum that offers good visual stimuli and that allows you to work in it. Try to choose subject areas in the museum that communicate the nature of its collection; research the background of these images both historically and for their visual development. Create a poster for a general audience that is simple and is printed in as few colors as possible. This project should be supported by research visuals and notes.

■ **From drawing to layout** The student has decided to contrast stylized historical costume with strong black and white imagery. This is developed from an initial thumbnail to more finished sketches, exploring the balance between reversed-out type, the drawn image, and white space (above).

design aimed at? What is their expected comprehension of visual matter? How are you going to hold their attention?

Basic lessons

The past is full of inspiration for the images you create today. Absorb all the visual arts, especially the way fashion has permeated decades of graphic imagery. Build a visual vocabulary to dip into for ideas. Organize your research, make use of the expertise of people such as librarians; study your target audience, their interests and lifestyles. Combine all this information into strong pieces of graphic communication.

V&A
YESTERDAY'S CLOTHES
TOMORROW'S DESIGN

Like many others CHRISTIAN

DIOR derived his **IDEAS** from

past DESIGNS. **see** what **YOU**

could be WEARING in the new

season at the V&A.

South Kensington ⊖

OPENING TIMES weekdays 10:00-17:50

WE SUGGEST adults £2·00 students and pensioners 50p

■ **Working on a theme**
The composition has been set now as equally divided black and white space. Final details on the design now have to be decided. This design approach relied strongly on the patterns created by the division of black and white and the loose, stylized fashion drawing.

■ **The poster** The student has produced a confident design (above) which fulfills the assignment in being produced in a single color – black – and has a strong period feel within a modern context.

T I P S

■ Go to the library to pinpoint your research, and plan your time there. Don't get diverted too often.
■ Always carry a sketchbook. As they are filled, file them for future reference.

■ Use the influences of the past constructively in your work.
■ Be inquisitive about all design and root out its source.
■ Study the fashions in design that each decade experiences.

From concept to visual: ORGANIZING YOUR THOUGHTS

So far, in the preceding sections, we have looked at numerous ways of expressing ideas visually, using a range of materials. You will now be more familiar with the techniques designers use to manipulate these media and form the best images for communication; you should understand how realism can be made to suit your design objectives; you know how to blend and use colors to visualize ideas. You can also use tints to make subtle backgrounds, render letterforms and indicate type by hand. Finding your way around the elements of design should now give you the confidence to apply these essential skills to the concept – the somewhat daunting prospect of the creation of original ideas.

Creativity is an elusive commodity, and no designer has cornered the market in it. Often the most experienced start by putting down on paper everything that relates to the subject at hand. There are a number of different methods that help in the organization of this research.

Making connections

To demonstrate this, let's take a product that might feature in an advertising campaign: milk. How many images and connections can you make from this single concept? Look at the health aspect; where does that lead? Who drinks milk? What about the range of products derived from milk? Consider its creation and the sequence of events leading up to its production. Look at its natural color. Consider the word "milk" itself and its counterparts in different languages. Think of the various locations ranging from the home to the office where you find milk. When is milk used? In what is it used? Explore the shapes of the containers milk is stored in and served in. What fun can you have with these related objects?

WILDLIFE PROJECT

Create an original visual concept for the Worldwide Fund for Nature that brings attention to the plight of endangered species of wild animals.

■ **Concept sheets** Your ideas should be expressed through sketches or written ideas that help you develop your own approach to the problem. Graphic design ideas work only when the concept is well thought out, appropriate to the subject, and self-explanatory. Use and develop the ideas on these early sheets that are likely to work for the project. The student has here sketched out a number of quick thoughts.

Continued on next page

■ Thumbnails When you have a concept that works for your project, test it in a wide range of applications. Examine illustrative approaches and experiment on how you can make your idea work visually.

■ Working up a visual approach After further research the student decided to use a humorous, illustrative style that would appeal to children while conveying a serious message. These colorful images would stand out in crowded space on billboards and poster sites.

■ **Finished visual** The finished poster design exploits the traditional illustrative approach but emphasizes the importance of the heading by cutting around it. Thus the important message is more likely to be read. The visuals seen here are produced using marker pens.

This is just the beginning. It is important to write down these thoughts, rather than relying on your memory because one idea will often obscure a previous thought. The words can form the hub of a wheel (page 120) around which the ideas can revolve. As each topic comes to mind, list all the interconnected thoughts that spring from this central source. Each one can be followed up separately, like the spokes of a wheel. Within a short space of time your central hub will be bristling with possible leads.

The elimination process

The next stage of development is to explore

the best of these emerging concepts. At this point you will also need to develop some visuals to establish quickly the viability of the idea. How skillful you are in picking out the most promising notion will probably determine the ultimate success of the design.

So what do you look for ? The idea should work when applied in a practical and functional design. Eliminate visual puns and clichés. These will only serve to make the originality of your work suspect. Colleagues are almost always prepared to voice their opinions – positive or negative. Ask them what their reactions are; invite criticism. Learning to listen to what people say about

■ **Following through** Using the same style as the parrot poster, these posters feature two other endangered species. In each, the clever heading is emphasized graphically by the cut-out shape. These posters are distinguished by their subtle use of cut-out shapes, which add individuality to the design.

Its official! Kar hasn't touched his airbrush in 3 weeks and the lions are dropping off like,er,lions.
THE WORLD WILDLIFE FU

Every year, hundreds of parrots die due to Man moving them from their natural habitat. We're trying to save this beautiful bird from extinction. Support us by telling your friends.
THE WORLD WILDLIFE FUND

SAVE OUR SNAKES!
We're trying to prevent our snakes from becoming a part of history
WWF

your work is, after all, part of your training. A casual word could hold the key to your design being successful.

Your problems are not over yet. You now have to put together a presentation visual that demonstrates why your idea is so strong. Not everyone is capable of appreciating a visual concept immediately, so you will have to augment it with a verbal explanation to persuade your client of the validity of your approach, supported by the careful thought and preparation that has gone into it.

Basic lessons
Ideas do not happen in a vacuum; they must

be sought out. Render the best ones in visual form, and if they do not stand up to scrutiny, scrap them now – don't go on trying to make them work. Seek out criticism and use it constructively, before making finished visuals. If you are listening attentively, you will not hear the same criticism more than once. It is also a good way to practice justifying your designs to a less than enthusiastic audience – but don't forget to acknowledge when adverse comments are valid.

■ **Promotional material**
The student has produced a range of promotional material to support the overall concept and to communicate the idea in graphic detail.

■ **Another approach**
to this project is seen in these masks and cards featuring endangered species. The twist in this concept is that each of the animals represented is a mixture of two animals. One combines a tiger and a frog, the other a zebra and a lion.

■ **Posters** The masks and cards are presented as flat images, displayed in a poster format. The linking of animals becomes a play on words with the invention of species like "Zebron." This graphic idea is fun but complex.

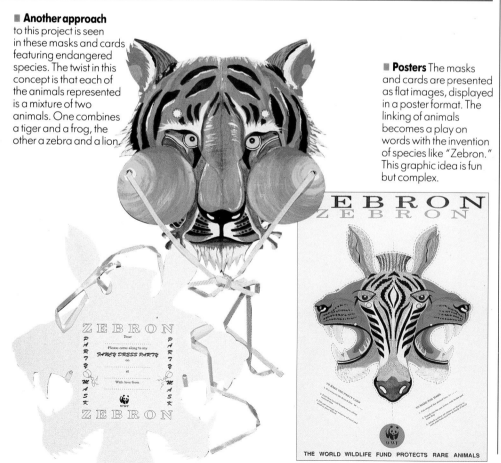

ZEBRON
ZEBRON

THE WORLD WILDLIFE FUND PROTECTS RARE ANIMALS

TIPS

■ Write down everything that relates to the subject. Don't rely on your memory.
■ Without a strong concept, your visual has no value.
■ Create a flow chart using a central hub with the spokes as routes for ideas.
■ Look for impartial criticism and use this in a professional manner.
■ Talk about your work as well as showing it.

From concept to visual: COORDINATED DESIGNS

■ **Research** The student has chosen to design a family of books that exploit cult images of recent decades, and has collected a series of familiar visual images relating to those years.

On many occasions the designer will be commissioned to produce a series of items to work together. These may be book jackets, each displaying an individual concept but being part of a series, perhaps. Or the products could be a range of cosmetics, where the individual components are bound together by a common design theme. This is a challenge to the designer, who can bring into play all the shades and subtleties of his main design theme.

Coordinated design means that each item is linked visually by layout, type, color, illustration, and style. Say, for example, you have designed one of these items using illustration, color, and type, and printed it on gold paper. The most striking element, the gold color, could become the unifying feature. The lettering, on the other hand, might be treated very simply in black or white, while the illustrations, although different for each application, would be drawn in a similar style. However, the way in which you present the design elements performs three important functions: first it sets the theme for the individual items; second, it is the factor that coordinates the items; and finally, it places your design in a context.

Coordinated design does not apply only to packaging. It affects magazines and news-

BOOK JACKET PROJECT

Design a series of three jackets for books (paperback) for your chosen author, deciding on type and illustrations, back and front covers. Plan the initial research: what is a book jacket's job? How is the series identifiable? What are the limitations on illustration, type, layout? What is the market? Write your own questions, then go out and find the answers. These should form part of your presentation. Although type and illustration may vary across the series, there should still be some identifiable link. Having read one book by John Smith, a customer will not want to hunt for hours for the next. How many books will be on display at one time? Will potential buyers be impressed by the look and feel of the cover, knowing nothing of the author? Remember, too, that what you put on the cover can enhance or detract from what is inside.

■ **Type** can also immediately evoke a period style. Here the student has sketched typical examples from each period.

papers, corporate image and its application, advertising campaigns, and direct mail promotions. Study a direct mail piece and you will see that the individual components – sales letter, application form, color leaflet – serve separate functions, yet are carefully coordinated to work as a group.

A book jacket is, essentially, another piece of packaging advertising a product and its manufacturer – the publisher. The jacket design must be stylish, be functional (i.e. tell you what the book is about), and perform at the point of sale – in other words, stand out among its competitors on the bookshop's crowded shelves. Sometimes the only visible part of the jacket is its spine, so the typography chosen here is very important.

Your concept for a jacket design may be influenced by other factors: the book's category – fiction or non-fiction – and the author's following – is this a first book or does he or she have a loyal band of eager readers? What is the time-scale and subject of the book? Is it set in the past, the present, or the future? Obviously, to answer these questions, you must have an idea of the book's contents, so don't be reluctant to ask the publisher for a synopsis, or even the full manuscript, if you feel it would add an extra dimension to your design.

■ **Coordinated designs** The three finished designs use cult figures from the decade, floating symbolically on a colored background, in the correct period style. The typeface remains constant throughout, with the exception of the word "style," which does little for the design. The pastel colors and consistency of image arrangement unite these three designs.

■ **Drawn images** The student has now expressed the images in various ways using graphic formulas suitable for a sequence of book jacket titles.

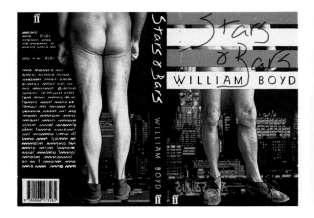

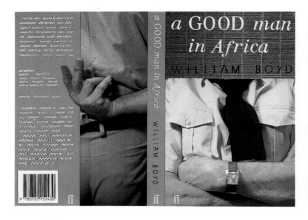

■ **Collage and montage**
These coordinated designs for three Flann O'Brien books make use of existing imagery, cunningly collaged into powerful illustrations. The use of carefully chosen cut letterforms carries the design through the spine and onto the back cover.

■ **Photography** The richness of William Boyd's work is well illustrated here using stage set photography taken by the student and made into color and black and white prints. These were arranged and photocopied in color to create the final designs.

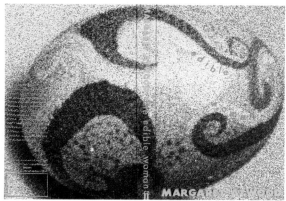

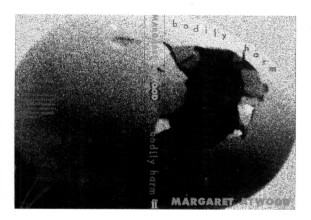

■ **Darkroom techniques**
In this series of designs
based around the same
theme, the student has
extracted a series of
powerful images using
darkroom techniques. A
very fast film has been
used to take the pictures,
which were printed on a
coarse grain paper.

■ **Computer** The design
theme for these books
echoes a TV documen-
tary style. Type running
off the top and bottom of
the pages implies the
movement of titles on a
television screen, while
the photographs link to
the documentary style of
writing and the content.
The student has added a
visual twist to the images
by extracting a portion
from the photographs
and regenerating it
through a graphics
computer. Images can
take on a completely
different form, and colors
can be changed and
added.

T I P S

■ Assess your design
elements with a view to
creating coordinated
designs: type, illustration,
color, range of colors,
layout, style, and the
material on which you are
printing.
■ Style sets the theme and
places your designs in
context.
■ You have a responsibility
to understand the subject
you are designing.
■ Check your presen-
tations and visuals for
spelling mistakes,
particularly in the product
name, the book's title, and
the client's company.

97

From concept to visual: USING PHOTOGRAPHY

■ Photographic references make a useful guide for practical illustration work. The sequence of events shown here can be simply photographed using an ordinary camera.

Some design tasks are solved swiftly and without fuss by adopting a strategy of planned photography. Because modern cameras produce good, clear photographs, it is often simpler for the designer to take reference photographs rather than struggle with an accurate drawing. For instance, you might imagine it is not difficult to make an accurate drawing of, say, a typewriter – it has a keyboard, a paper carrier, and is fairly square in shape. However, try to put the image on paper – how many keys does it have? In how many rows? And you have barely started to draw! So, why not take a photo of a typewriter instead? This can be

done either by finding a suitable image in your reference collection, by using a Polaroid camera, or by shooting it on 35mm film which you can process yourself or have developed locally, often in a matter of hours.

These photographs or references become the basis on which copy drawings or enlarged, traced drawings are made. Most design studios and art schools are equipped with a machine for enlarging or reducing drawings. It has a glass work surface and is operated somewhat like a photographic enlarger. A light shining through or onto the photograph to be enlarged is projected through a lens onto the glass surface. By

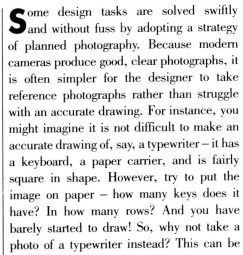

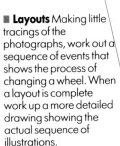

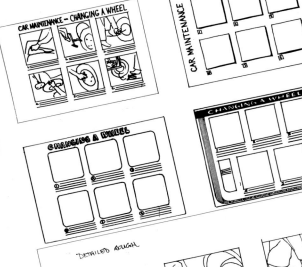

■ Layouts Making little tracings of the photographs, work out a sequence of events that shows the process of changing a wheel. When a layout is complete work up a more detailed drawing showing the actual sequence of illustrations.

moving the lens up or down, you can trace the image to the required size.

The second method is to use a scaling grid. Over the area of the photo you want enlarged, draw a grid divided into equal-sized squares, say, ten squares by ten squares. On a separate piece of paper rule another grid, also made up of 100 equal squares, but to the size you want the final drawing to be. Taking each individual square on the picture, you can now transfer the images contained within that square, drawing them in the equivalent square on the larger grid. Once you have systematically transferred the entire area of the photograph, you will find that the new

drawing is a scaled-up version. The same method in reverse will give scaled down images. For those with access to a photocopier, the same result can be achieved instantly at the touch of a button.

Photography is particularly helpful when developing drawings that represent a stage-by-stage sequence of events. Here, drawings are preferable to photographs, as they are clearer and easier to adapt to fit the other graphic elements. At this stage you can consider type, illustrations, and the colors to be printed.

■ **Finished artwork** for this instruction sequence can now be drawn using technical pens, with the main information drawn in simple linear form. A fine technical pen will be necessary for this work. Mechanical tints can be overlaid for shading. These tints are available in different tones and are simply cut from a sheet and applied to the areas you wish. The copy is typeset and positioned in accordance with your layout.

CAR MAINTENANCE

NUMBER 7 - CHANGING A WHEEL

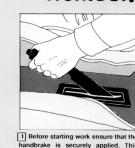

1 Before starting work ensure that the handbrake is securely applied. This will prevent the car moving and possibly falling off the jack.

2 Jack the car up on the relevant side. Stop just before the tyre leaves contact with the ground.

3 Loosen the wheel nuts with a wheel brace and remove them. If the wheel has a tendency to rotate, lower the jack.

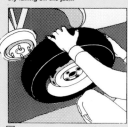

4 Jack the wheel clear of the ground and then remove it from the hub. Take care not to damage the threads.

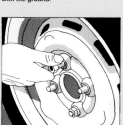

5 Install the spare wheel and replace the nuts finger tight. Finish tightening with the wheelbrace.

6 Inflate the tyre to the correct pressure and lower the vehicle to the ground. Take the damaged tyre for repair.

T I P S

■ Plan photography as a drawing aid.
■ Images can be traced from photography.
■ Keep a piece of paper between your hand and your work.
■ Make each component of artwork separately.
■ Remember to add cropping marks to guide the cutting.

From concept to visual: ARTWORKING YOUR DESIGN

Technical pens are used for artworking, and for creating key-line shapes which the printer uses as an edge guide for laying a flat area of color, a tint, or solid black. Technical pens come in various thicknesses depending on the required weight of line. Because this line work will be reproduced in the final print, accuracy is paramount. To keep the work clean, slip a sheet of paper between your hand and the working surface.

Other technical supports help in creating clean artwork images: instant rubdown type for headings should be applied to separate thin surfaces and then mounted on to the artwork. This avoids making mistakes on the actual artwork. In fact, there is no reason why all components should not be made separately and brought together on the artwork board. Manufacturers of rub-down lettering also produce a range of tones, ranging from very dark gray to light dots. These are specially designed for tonal illustrations that can be printed without complicated techniques.

Basic print methods

Although the printer can interpret most artworks and produce a printing plate from what is supplied, he is still governed by the printing process itself. If your design is reproduced in a single color and you require tonal effects, then clearly there has to be a method in which tones can be applied at the same time as the solid areas are being printed. The ink used is always consistently the same color. Therefore, the color has to be broken down into lighter tints on your artwork or by specifying to the printer. These tints are simply larger or smaller dots printed closer together or farther apart.

If you examine a piece of newsprint under a magnifying glass you will see that all the tonal areas of photographs and illustrati consist of different dots of ink. It is possible for the printer to treat your material in the same way, but to keep control of the exact tonal effect, you can apply your own rubdown mechanical tints. The printer will then use these in the same way as he does those he makes himself. Much modern print is made up by using this optical effect of mixing dots to create the illusion of light and shade.

Design for two-color artwork

The best way to understand how print can be manipulated by design is to start very simply with a two-color piece. The subject is to be a simple poster for a local event. Begin by creating alternative designs in the two colors. For this exercise, keep to the same two colors

TECHNICAL PENS
PROJECT

Create the following pieces of test work with a selection of technical pens and a steel ruler. Draw a large rectangle with a medium thickness pen. Switching to a fine pen, draw another rectangle that fits within the first; leave an equal space between the fine and the medium line on four sides. Repeat this to create a third inner rectangle.

Draw the same sized rectangle with a heavy border. Divide this into a large number of small squares, and draw in the diagonals for all the squares with the fine pen.

Draw the same sized rectangle with a heavy border. Divide the space vertically or horizontally into very narrow equal spaces, and draw in the lines with a fine pen. Fill in each alternate space with ink and brush.

Draw the same sized rectangle with a heavy border. Measure out a rectangle to fit just inside the outer border with a medium pen, but do not complete the corners. Now add them in as curves with a technical pen and a compass.

■ **1** This drawing was produced using two different weights of technical pen: extra fine for the two inner lines and slightly thicker for the outer rule. You will need to work at least twice as large as the reduced images shown here.

■ **2** For this drawing you will need just one thickness of pen: medium fine. The outer thick rule is created using two parallel lines filled in with a fine brush and ink. The criss-cross effect must be drawn extremely accurately to ensure that all lines cross at the correct point.

■ **3** The lines drawn here were made up from parallel fine lines and filled in using a fine brush and ink. The initial drawing needs to be made in pencil with extreme accuracy. Check this carefully before using the pen and ink.

■ **4** The outer border was created using parallel lines, filled in with ink. The inner border was first drawn as a rectangle in pencil. The corner curves were then drawn in pencil using a compass. Then, using a ruling pen compass or a compass with a technical pen holder, the curves were inked in. Lines were then drawn up in the same thickness pen to meet with the corner curves.

1

2

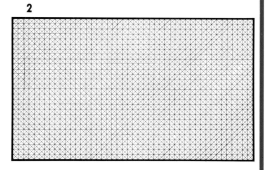

3

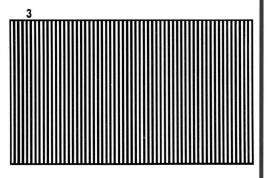

4

TWO-COLOR
PROJECT

Take a local event. Decide on the information to be displayed. Create a number of alternative thumbnail sketches using two colors. Select one of the thumbnail sketches as the basis for development, and create a larger, more finished visual. Create separated artworks of the two colors, ensuring accuracy and perfect registration.

■ Color design ideas

The first roughs for a local event are shown here. They make use of different layout designs using two colors, red and black. Tints of these two colors have been added in places, but the choice of colors could be more adventurous.

for working out alternative designs. If you choose black and one color, that is what you will get in the final print. You can have tones and shades, of course, but they will be out of the one color. However, choosing blue and yellow and overlaying the blue onto the yellow will result in a third color – green. Modern printing inks can be viewed as sheets of translucent film. Blue film plus yellow gives you green. A similar effect can be achieved by using the basic print colors. Two separate pieces of artwork, one for the parts of the design to be printed in blue, and one for yellow are overlaid to print as the third color. But how do you go about converting your design into printable artwork?

Registration Artwork for multi-color printing should be produced on separate overlay sheets for each color. These need to have accurate registration marks, as they will be detached by the printer to make a separate printing plate for each color.

■ **Drawing to a manageable size** The design will need to be drawn accurately, remembering that each color needs separate artwork. Alternative designs can be produced to give you or your client a number of choices. Once a decision has been made, a full-size drawing needs to be created as guidance for the artwork: The design elements can be drawn separately and pieced together if you wish.

■ **Separated artwork**
Using your visual as a guide draw the elements for the first color in black on artboard. The second color elements are drawn in black on the overlay.

Separating the artwork

Assemble the elements for the design to be artworked: illustrations, photographs, type, etc. Some elements, like type or small line illustrations, may need to be sized up – made larger or smaller to the correct size for the artwork. This is not difficult but requires a special piece of equipment, the PMT camera (Photo Mechanical Transfer), which prints what is in reality a high quality photocopy of the image (also called a velox). The correctly sized PMT is then pasted onto the artwork or the overlay. Plan out which areas will be represented in which color. The larger areas such as backgrounds are usually positioned on the base art board. The overlay carrying

the second color overprinted material is attached to it with tape. The third color will appear where the images on the overlay (the second color) overlap the images on the base (the main color). If you specify it, the black line and black typesetting can also be printed in one of your three colors or reversed out of a color, the letterforms printing in white. Draw the whole artwork in pencil on your board. Using this as a guide, draw up the base artwork for one color, in black. Put in the registration marks. Position your overlay over the base artwork, and tape them together securely, aligning and copying the registration marks. Now draw in and position the second color artwork.

■ Printing in color
From your two separate sheets of black artwork the printer will make individual printing plates. These are run separately through the press using any color printing ink you specify. When the two plates have run through the press you will end up with a printed image in two colors.

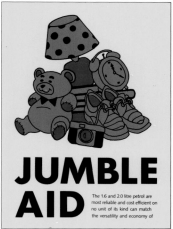
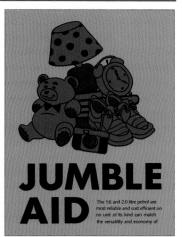
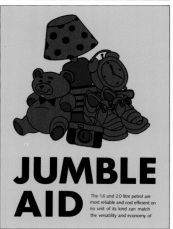
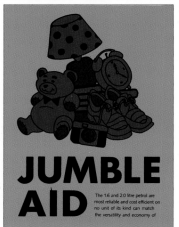

TIPS

■ Begin by working several ideas in a combination of the same two colors.
■ Different overlay effects will give a third color.
■ Keep your design simple, as you will need to separate the elements for artwork.

Marking up artwork for the printer

These are the basic techniques the designer uses to make up artwork for different printed colors. One of the most essential skills necessary to achieve the desired printed effect, however, is the ability to communicate your instructions to the color separation house and printer, precisely and accurately, and in a language they understand. Full color illustrations can be indicated on the artwork in the shape and size of the image and outlined in blue (the camera will fail to pick this up). Those illustrations can then be supplied on separate sheets.

On receiving your artwork, the printer converts the work into a printing plate by a photographic process; the black artwork and the full-color images are worked on separately and then brought together on the printing plate. The blue lines are used to register the image accurately in position.

The key to good print results is accurately positioning all the elements on layout and overlays. Mark up the print specifications on another overlay − tracing paper or layout paper, not the artwork. For safety's sake, you can show on this overlay what is required, as a color visual, particularly if the directions to the printer are complex.

You will also need to specify colors that are to be placed in between line work. For example, if you have an outline letterform that is to be filled in with color, it is probably better to indicate this as a visual, in addition to your color specification, than to hope the printer will get it right and risk incurring reproofing at your own expense.

Color specification

You can specify color in two ways. The first method is to pick your colors from the Pantone (color system) specifier and quote the numbers for each of the colors. These can then be matched by the printer to the process colors: yellow, magenta, cyan, and black. These three colors, plus black, represent the total range the printer has to produce four-color print.

The second way of specifying your colors is by means of tint charts. Choose the appropriate color from the chart, read off the percentages of the individual colors that will make up the color you want, and give the printer the specific instructions to mix the depth of color needed, for example: 100% process yellow + 50% magenta = orange.

These instructions will be given to specify color from black artwork, and for backgrounds and in-filling. Full color illustrations and photographs will be reproduced as you see them unless you instruct otherwise.

Basic lessons

Single color work can be improved with mechanical tints to give a tonal quality to work that would otherwise look flat. A third color can be created from two colors by cunning artwork and positioning of overlays.

Marking up artwork is a precise business, so combine visual and written instructions, but on an overlay, not the actual artwork. A blue line on artwork is used to indicate the position of separate color illustrations.

■ **1 Tint charts** The three "process" print colors are magenta, cyan, and yellow. Different percentages of these can theoretically make any color. You only need to specify the percentages of each, which you will find on a tint chart, and the printer will do the rest.

■ **2 Pantone** With the Pantone system you just choose the color you want from a full range of catalogued colors, shown on the Pantone Color Specifier.

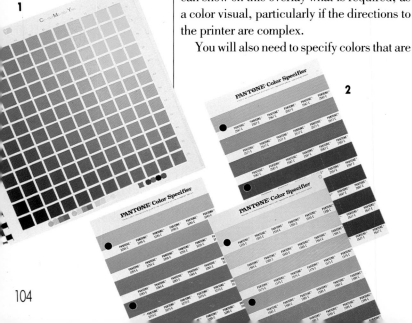

1

2

AIRBRUSHED ARTWORK-EASILY DAMAGED

AIRBRUSHED ARTWORK-EASILY DAMAGED

3

4

From artwork to printed image
1 The full color airbrushed artwork. Negatives in the three process colors plus black will be made from this.
2 The overlay shows the pasted up type in position and the black border. Note the registration and cutting marks.
3 Another overlay is created on layout or flimsy paper. Here the designer shows how the type is to appear white out of the background at the top, and specifies color for the letters at the bottom and the border.
4 The finished printed record sleeve. See how the instructions have been followed.

T I P S

■ Your instructions must always be clear and precise.
■ Blue key-lines on artwork indicate the position of separately supplied illustrations or photographs.
■ PMTs will enlarge or reduce line or half-tones.
■ Use an overlay to mark up your print instructions.
■ Sketch out complex visual instructions where this might help the printer.
■ Only black and white artwork needs to be marked up for color; illustrations and photographs in full color will be reproduced as seen.

From concept to visual: COMPUTER GRAPHICS

Computers are now commonly used to assist graphic designers to create and produce ideas. The vast range of available programs let the designer and illustrator carry out certain types of design work without wasting time on some repetitive tasks. Illustrations can be created either by using a specially-designed pen and electronic pad, or a "mouse" – a small hand operated unit.

The pen allows the artist to draw in different line thicknesses on the pad. The image drawn is reproduced on screen, and many other graphic devices can be introduced. For example, tones can be laid in position and colors can be added. Many more interesting effects can also be imposed on the drawing.

The advantages of carrying out this work on a computer are speed, accuracy, and definition and the opportunity to experiment and reinterpret. For instance, many programs offer a range of typefaces. The designer can therefore set the text in one typeface and then display alternatives on screen instantly. The type can be reversed or distorted, and displayed in color. With traditional hand rendering, work like this needs skill and dedication, and a great deal of time.

The same applies to simple illustrations. They can be created as rough drawings on screen and can then be developed using the computer's drawing facilities, or inbuilt options from the program menu.

Computers also offer a reasonably accurate interpretation of what the final image will look like. The finished image can be made up in the colors required and in alternative colors with a few simple operations.

The versatility of computers also allows the manipulation of graphic images in the layout process. Each item can be produced on screen and patched together into different

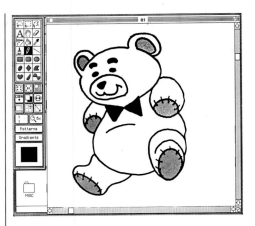

■ Illustration and graphics on computers
An illustration can be created on computer either by tracing it from a drawing on paper, using a light pen or mouse, or drawing it directly on the screen in a freehand program. Imperfections in drawing can be removed by enlarging the screen image, and tones can be added from the program menu. The drawings can be laid together on the screen as though they were loose images on a drawing board. They can then be moved together and combined into a larger illustration.

■ **Distortions, enlargements and trick effects** Graphics programs have many in-built facilities which allow you to manipulate your work in a variety of ways.

■ **Choice of type** The choice of typefaces available makes it very easy for you to see how the words relate to the design.

JUMBLE SALE

JUMBLE SALE

JUMBLE SALE

JUMBLE SALE

JUMBLE SALE

■ **Reversing out and color** Simple commands can reverse out an image or change it into one of the many colors available.

layouts with different emphasis and proportion to each of the elements. This means many layouts can be created using the same graphic input.

For any basic design the computer is an ideal tool, but it is also useful for more complex design problems. Sophisticated computers allow complicated imagery to be created. Highly skilled work can be done after only a minimum of training on the machine. For example, photographic images can be retouched and illustrations simulating airbrush effects can be created. Three-dimensional programs offer even greater scope, and specialist video cameras or scanning equipment allow found images to be displayed on screen.

However, the screen image is only part of the process. Images need to be retained and produced on paper to display to clients. Many computer printers offer good quality black and white reproductions, and some offer reasonable color quality.

Probably the most significant reason why computers have become so important is that no actual artwork needs to be made before designs are printed. This is because the disk that retains the design includes all the information that a printer needs to create the finished printed item by litho printing.

What you must remember is that none of these images can be created unless you first have the knowledge and skills of traditional design. In fact, the better you are at creating drawings and designs the more adept you will become when using a computer. The computer is no substitute for skill, it is just a support.

JUMBLE SALE at the Queens Hall in Romford on Saturday March 23rd

1990

■ **Computer collage** In a process similar to collage, your individual images can be brought together on screen to create an integrated design.

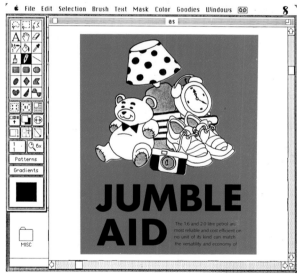

Versatility and speed

The computer makes the process of creating a layout much more speedy. It is a simple matter to enlarge or reduce type, move illustrations around, or change the overall proportions. Color can also be displayed, so that you can see what your design will look like in its finished form.

TIPS

- Designs can be interpreted with versatility and speed.
- Ideas can be explored with reduced effort.
- Typefaces can be rried and easily substituted from the choices available.

Elements can be displayed on screen and patched together in different layouts.

Computers can eliminate the need for artwork.

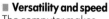

109

Chapter Three: COMMERCIAL PRACTICE

Now that you have discovered how to interpret a design assignment, explore this for ideas and generate a number of options through to a final conclusion. You have realized the different potential of different media, and you know the professional standards required to present your ideas.

You now need to become familiar with the graphic design industry and the various opportunities it offers. Each sector requires a different approach. What a design consultancy will be looking for, an advertising agency may avoid. Your own temperament, likes, and dislikes will govern your choice of direction.

You may be more interested in creating images for their own sake, or you may be better suited to the creation of promotional ideas. You may be interested in a specific area, such as typography or illustration, which you wish to develop and exploit. This chapter, with its range of different assign-

■ **Right** A student's finished layout for the cover of a new magazine.

Right An innovative display idea for the promotion of wrapping paper.

ments, gives you an opportunity of testing yourself with realistic commercial jobs which cover most of the graphic disciplines.

Each area of work requires its own special approach. It is important to test yourself by undertaking each of the assignments, as your understanding and your interpretation should teach you to recognize those areas where you excel.

Look at the individual projects and compare the methods and ideas used by each individual student. These reinforce the personality involved in creating graphic design ideas. Now you should interpret the assignments in your own way. You are also looking for the route that will carry you into a fulfilling area of creativity.

The creative professionals who have contributed to this chapter offer sound advice and a variety of approaches. The graphic design industry employs a wide range of personalities, from the efficient artworker to the most colorful thinkers. However, it always needs individuals who are dedicated and original, whatever their chosen discipline may be.

Corporate design: SEMINAR

IAN LOGAN, head of his own international graphic design studio.

I not only run a graphic design studio, but have also for many years marketed my own products around the world. Unlike most designers I am aware from both sides of the desk of what design should do. This may make me a little more sympathetic than I should be when taking instructions from a client, but when you realize that there is a warehouse full of expensive products, all of which are occupying an expensive space, you begin to share something of the nervousness that the businessman or manufacturer feels.

"a student of graphic design today should be visually hungry."

I believe a student of graphic design today should be visually hungry. In my case, when I left art school, not as a graphic designer but as a textile designer, I was influenced by the revival of blues music in the Fifties and Sixties. This led me to America, where I saw graphics that I found unbelievable. The American railway graphics of this time featured the Rock Island line. I was amazed both by the existence of a company that I had only heard of in a song and by the stunning graphics used by the line's owner, who wanted to shout his name across the state.

Images of this kind came from a pride in the service or product they were creating. I have always seen the chequered flags and heraldic symbols of World War II fighter planes, echoing the knights of the Middle Ages, as linked to the concept of logos. Such symbols, although lost to us today, had great meaning to the public in the past.

I have always allowed myself to be influenced by the best images from the past. From old railway posters and artists such as Tom Purvis and Frank Newbourne through to modern-day inspirations such as Milton Glaser, all these enrich my visual language.

Students should absorb

what there is to be seen as well as concentrate on creating images themselves. In this way they offer the world of design a dedication to quality.

The designer/client relationship

Naturally, when dealing with a client you are not just dealing with your own sense of image-making. You are dealing with a personality, so it is wise to build up a relationship with this individual. Try to get the precise feel of his market and always give him your very best.

It is a common fault to assume that clients and the public need educating, when often they just need good design standards. Design should be just as good for something costing a pound or a dollar as something costing thousands. The same integrity should go into the design of the cheaper item as goes into that of the most expensive.

In my view, the study of design is becoming too precious. I believe that studying the visual arts, and especially graphic design, should help people find themselves in all manner of business careers. Once the student has learned to enjoy looking — and this experience is in itself

■ **Above** Early 20th century American railroad companies devised effective corporate liveries.

fulfilling – then how they apply this in terms of their career is not so important. It can be just as exciting to be a buyer of design as to be a designer. In fact, standards of design might improve if more people were conscious of the visual language. Realistically, not all graphic design students will become graphic designers, but what they will learn will be invaluable for a multitude of careers.

"Design should be just as good for something costing a pound or a dollar as something costing thousands."

Once this has been realized, the whole of today's design education can be viewed as an extension of the normal education our young people receive.

When advising students about their careers I would say that they should enjoy first being creative people and absorbing images, and then, if design is really what captivates them, they will naturally be drawn into some aspects of the business.

There is no better motivator than an enthusiasm and love for image making.

My own visual enthusiasm led me into manufacturing my own products, which range from soaps and luxury toiletries to home-made products such as confectionery. Each of these products is packaged in a tin box. What really makes these products desirable is the graphics on them. Let me return to my point about integrity of design. My range of products is fun to create because I involve the best illustrators and designers that are around. It gives me great joy to give a brief to an illustrator who returns with an image that is ten times better than I had anticipated. I think the inspiration comes from us both. They know that I am seeking excellent design, and this acts as a spur to their integrity. If this concept was used in all areas of design, where client and designer strive for the best, then the future would be bright.

■ **Right** World War II bombers often carried distinctive "heraldic" images

Corporate design

Corporate identity is a major part of design work, and although there are no straightforward formulas for the creation of good images, there are some guidelines that I think students ought to be aware of. The first thing you must realize when creating a logo or image is that what you are starting is something that should last. To do this you have to recognize

"It is the designer's job to assess design objectively: not just his own work, but every design he sees."

some of the classics that have survived and understand why they have. I was recently involved in the redevelopment of the image of a major institution which some years before had created a design based on the infinity symbol. The institution is a famous business school, and although the intellectual idea behind this symbol is sound, for anyone to associate this sign with its meaning and then to apply that to the school itself needs a written explanation.

The reason why famous

logos such as those used by Hoover or Coca Cola last, despite the fickle fashions of design, is because of their direct message. Even so, I am sure that over the years they have been slightly adjusted to accommodate new thinking. This visual adjustment happens more slowly than you could imagine, so you are unaware of the change. Some very famous logos have been changed to their detriment. It is not always necessary to update a logo but it is necessary to create a tight structure for it to operate in. In this way it cannot be tampered with by new mem-

bers of staff trying to make their mark on a company, and everyone within that company understands there is a design manual to follow. What most established images need is a strict book which says, for example: You do not use 15 shades of green, you use this one.

It is sometimes good for a design business to be handed the job of redesigning a famous corporate image, but I feel that if you cannot find any reason why the existing logo should be changed, then that is what you tell the client. It is the designer's job to assess design objectively:

not just his own work, but every design he sees. Because a logo can go out of fashion, it is important that the designer also take this into account in the early stages of the design.

"Designers try to be too clever sometimes; in my view the key to good corporate design is simple communication."

With world-famous logos you need only to glimpse the name to associate it immediately with the product. That is what I would call a classic logo and a design that works. Designers try to be too clever sometimes; in my view the key to good corporate design is simple communication. The designer must be wary of producing something merely fashionable, unless of course it is for a fashion shop. But even then it must have lasting qualities.

In short, a corporate identity should stand on its own feet and need no further information. It should reflect the strength of the company, and the public should know exactly what that is.

■ **Above** This American park warden's badge carries a logo that clearly illustrates the job.

Corporate design: INTRODUCTION

The following commercial projects explore corporate design. This type of work often forms the major part of studio design activity, but specialist graphic design studios have emerged to undertake this important work, thus assuming responsibility for the shaping of a company or organization's public image.

Corporate images have a great influence on the overall success of a company. They range from a logo – in effect a company signature which can be applied to every aspect of its printed or visual material – to a house style, which includes everything from interior design and decor to company livery and uniforms.

The principal requirement of a logo is that it should fully reflect the company's market position. A company selling direct to the public would present itself by using a visually appropriate image which would immediately identify the supplier with its chosen market. The logo would enable the company to position itself visually alongside its competitors, and also help it to appear the most professional and attractive supplier within that market sector. Logos are used in this way right across the commercial spectrum.

The logo can be incorporated, with further design work, into stationery, transportation, and signs that indicate the company's presence or locate its points of sale. It can also be used in press advertising – in many cases in black and white. It is therefore important that a broad range of possible applications be taken account of in the early stages of the image's creation, to ensure its consistent effectiveness in widely differing media.

Problem solving

The first problem the graphic designer faces is how to convey, through a symbol or symbolic image, the essence and personality of a company or organization. A designer commissioned to undertake this type of work must always evaluate the problem within its context. The design of a logo or a company image must be dictated by the client's requirements and the designer's research. A client may favor particular themes, and these are important influences on the design. But the priority should always be to obtain the most appropriate market image, however different this may become from the original concept. It is a matter of interpreting the client's subjective view while taking advantage of the research material.

Much of the problem solving in corporate design work relies on thorough research and intelligent market decisions, followed by good visual interpretation. Effort spent at this stage in trying to assess what is an appropriate image for your client is invaluable. Look at other logos, especially those of competitors, as these will give you the essence of the marketplace and help you avoid the trap of duplication. Aim to identify the individual personality of your client, but note that this can be achieved only by looking and talking to as many as possible of the people who are involved in the shaping of the company's products or services.

The sense of achievement that is to be gained from this kind of work is fulfilling in

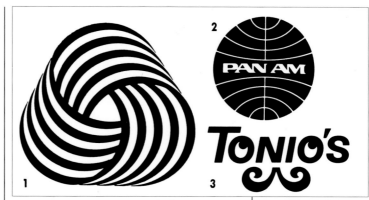

■ **Classic logos**
Successful logos can be created by image alone, as in the deceptively simple logo of the International Wool Secretariat by Francesco Saroglia (1), by combining type and image, as in the familiar Pan Am logo by Joseph Montgomery (2), or by clever use of punning typography, as in the Saul Bass & Associates' logo for Tonio's Restaurant (3).

■ Study the client's requirements carefully.
■ Talk to the personalities involved in the company.
■ Seek out an image that reflects the personality of the company.
■ Do not imitate other images.
■ Bear in mind that your design has to be applied in many forms.
■ Simplicity will make the image more versatile and your design memorable.

many ways. Having created a new and original image, the designer is often in an advantageous position should there be a need for further development of the client's graphics. Once the difficulties and hard work of creating a working image have been overcome, it is very satisfying to retain control of the growth of the graphic material required by the client. As a client's organization grows in stature, so does the work of the graphic designer.

Basic lessons

Consider the following projects. Marketing guidelines are set and then fixed as each project develops. The instructions should be considered not in terms of the restrictions they place on the work but in terms of how they assist the creative process. At this point a client often indicates a preferred direction by including his or her ideas in the instructions.

As you research your project you will learn how to relate various forms of information to the instructions. You may look at the products in a historical context. You may refer to your knowledge of art history. Watch for relevant visual information in your picture research. It is also very useful to establish at the outset a collection of cuttings and interesting ephemera. This material can be filed in scrapbooks under categories such as logos, interesting type images, illustration styles, and so on. Such a collection will allow you to compare graphic design of the past with current work.

Finally, look for a unique way to apply this information, bearing in mind that a single image can be varied by the choice of technique to convey a range of meanings. At this stage you should be able to unite within a single design the techniques and ideas you have developed so far.

LOGO DESIGN ASSIGNMENT

The company name is Peabody and Crump, a fictional graphic and art materials supplier. A national company with outlets throughout the country, this old-established firm has been supplying quality materials for over a century. Because its name is well established, the company would like to see a logo that incorporates the letters of its name rather than an abstract form. The task is to create a logo that gives the company a modern image but also conveys the nature of its business.

Design requirements
Create a logo that can be used for the overall promotion of the company. There should be the facility to print the logo in color and black and white or in a single color. The logo design will be applied to letterheads, business cards, and other stationery, and will be used on displays in the company's retail outlets.

Technical requirements
The logo should be produced to be printed in litho. It will also need to be flexible enough for application on both display material and the product range – for example, on layout pads. It is to be reproduced on stock letterhead paper, standard size. A maximum of three colors should be used in the final print.

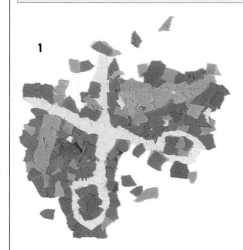

1

■ **1 Finding an idea** The student first experimented with some graphic materials by cutting paper to form an illustration. Ideas began to emerge – from the shape of the scissors to the different shapes cut out of the paper.

2

■ **2 Identifying the shapes** Developing the theme of scissors and cut paper the student then drew up a number of interlocking shapes that echoed the cruciform of the scissors and the now controlled drawn shapes.

PEABODY&CRUMP

■ **3 Shapes and letterforms** The next approach was to integrate letterforms and to toy with the idea of drawings of graphic instruments surrounding them.

4

■ **4 Organizing the logo** The student began with a logo in upper case letters and progressed by changing the colors, creating a more harmonious balance, and by introducing lower case letters. Changes in the ampersand and the color arrangement show how subtle manipulation can result in positive changes.

Most businesses, small or large, require a trading image, and this will be present on all the printed material used by a company. The purpose is to establish a distinctive and appropriate label that separates a business from its competitors.

The most common application of the logo is on letterheads, invoices, receipt books, and business cards. Its use may also extend to the livery, packaging, product labeling, and press advertisements.

Making a successful logo

It is not wise to pluck images from thin air in the hope of producing an image of stature. You need to look at the products or services the client provides as a means of directing your design thoughts. The best logos are simple to read, speak for themselves and the product or service, and do not need a complicated accompanying note to help them convey their message. The only planning a logo needs is after its creation, when the designer no longer has it under his or her control. This is achieved by creating a design manual.

The design manual

Most small companies will not need a complex book of instructions on how to apply their logo, but they may need guidance to help them specify colors for printing, and the size at which the logo should be displayed. A simple grid can be overlaid on the logo, so that it can be enlarged for use in larger formats. The manual will also give directions for the angle at which the logo should appear, and to get this right horizontal and vertical registration lines are used. The larger the company the tighter the manual. If the design is to be used by personnel in separate locations, it is important that the design be clearly specified to cover any application.

Continued on next page

■ **Alternative designs**
Each of these designs incorporated something different. The main changes were to the letters b and m, and the ampersands, represented as crosses, were treated with different techniques.

■ **Further design applications** The logo now offered a design style for use in many complementary pieces of packaging and point of sale material.

Critique

The commission indicated that the company's name should feature strongly in the design. The student's comprehension of this directed him to a typographical design early in this project. Although the letterforms that emerged were expressly chosen for their traditional appearance, an interesting twist is to apply illustrative devices to each of the letterforms. Taking a type image as a design motif itself is central to the creation of many logos. Once you are able to focus on the image the type forms convey in themselves, you can apply these in other forms.

In this project the student imposed a characteristic of the company's product range on individual letter or character forms derived from the name itself. The experimentation with color and form took the design through logical phases of embellishment to the finished logo. Further experimentation is possible, but the logo has achieved a firm design solution that allows a great deal of flexibility, and it can be inventively used in part or whole in a number of other design applications.

■ **Roughs for letterheads** Retaining the earlier theme of the scissors, the diagonal lines were used to crisscross the design area and link with the Peabody logo applied in different forms. These roughs were produced loosely, without the logo being reproduced accurately.

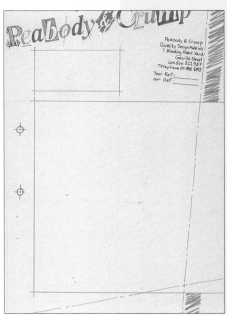

■ **Coordinated designs** A larger presentation visual for the letterheads was then produced. Even at this stage the logo was still evolving and the ampersand was reintroduced. Designs for other stationery were then produced to link with the theme created by the letterhead.

T I P S

■ Establish the exact nature of the logo's application.
■ How much flexibility is there in using color?
■ Methods of print can influence the design.
■ The logo should directly promote the nature of the company's business.
■ Make sure that the finished logo can be applied to all the specified material.
■ Good design can be practical and straightforward.

Corporate design: CORPORATE IDENTITY

The first task for the designer with a corporate image commission is to carry out research in the marketplace, establishing where similar products are sold and how the public responds to them. You could devise a questionnaire which sounds out consumers' attitudes to the products, and allows them to be critical. Investigate who buys the products and how they feel these should be presented. Write down a list of the areas you need to evaluate. Include in this list the pricing of individual items. How are different price ranges displayed? How are the graphics related to these prices? Does an inexpensive item look any cheaper because of the graphic formulas used? What colors are used to imply quality, and are there any surprises in the way in which they are used?

The owner of the My Beautiful Lingerie shops (right) has, as a result of her own experience in this market, her own clear ideas. These help formulate a partial picture of the type of purchaser of lingerie to whom she aims to appeal. The locations of her shops indicates a fairly affluent clientele of educated, professional women who have clear ideas of how they want to look. They demand well-tailored and attractive undergarments. She aims to offer them well-fitted, well-designed lingerie from an extensive range. The designer will recognize the strong input the shop's owner can make into this project, so his or her responsibility is to establish right from the start the strengths and weaknesses of the company as perceived by the owner, and how she wishes to see her business projected.

Developing a concept

So far there is no indication of any visual routes or roots. In fact, there are as yet no visual constraints, so that the designer has a considerable choice of approaches. You

CORPORATE IMAGE
ASSIGNMENT

Design a house style and a corporate image to promote a fast-growing chain of lingerie shops. The aim is to create a unique and appealing look that suits this specific market. Market research is to be based on the client's own experience and an independent study of the customer base.

The company name is "My Beautiful Lingerie," a name that appeared in 1987, when the first shop opened. They specialize in good quality, stylish lingerie, an area of clothing and fashion that has long been overlooked, and it is the company's intention, therefore, to establish a highly professional marketplace for itself. Although they are of high quality, the garments are not excessively expensive.

Design requirements
The company has not yet established a strong corporate image. The project's aim is therefore to devise a styling that can be applied to every aspect of the company's public image, from stationery to the internal and external appearance of the shops. Shopping bags and packaging materials are also to be considered.

Technical requirements
The format for printed material should comply with conventional paper sizes and print methods. Full-color printing is available if the design demands it.

■ **Student B**
1 Before attempting any visual ideas the student created a flow chart of ideas.

2 From the central word "underwear" the student developed ideas, ranging from statues to modern interpretations of classic images.

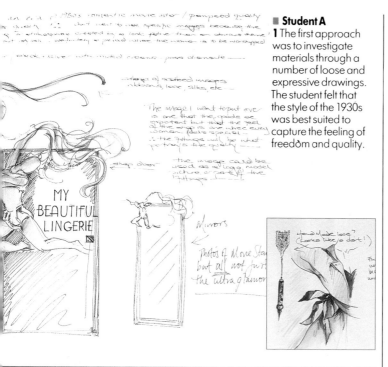

1 The first approach was to investigate materials through a number of loose and expressive drawings. The student felt that the style of the 1930s was best suited to capture the feeling of freedom and quality.

could start by thinking about the ideas and external stimuli that influence the personalities who are central to the research, and take into account the images and lifestyles with which they are likely to identify. These key personalities are the owner of the shops, her staff, and, most important of all, the customers. Construct a profile of each of these people, noting their income bracket, their type of work, and the kind of fashions they relate to. You can initiate this process by researching lifestyles in relevant magazines and similar sources.

An alternative, more adventurous route is to give free rein to your own visual fantasies, allowing the image to be shaped by your personal visual preferences. At this stage the final image is still of little importance.

Creating images

The two approaches shown here demonstrate the different starting points chosen by the designers concerned. Their concepts vary widely and although their methods of

■ **Developing a concept**
Found pictures and images will assist in pinpointing lifestyles, historic periods and the techniques of applying images. Written notes to accompany these will help you to identify their links with your project.

working are dissimilar, it is clear that each approach is necessary and appropriate to the solution that they seek. This point is crucial to the projects' evolution and possibly to their potential success. This is the most difficult

Continued on next page

stage for the designer, who must think, even this early, about the possible outcome of concepts and ideas.

A note of caution. As the designer, you must be able to justify all your design ideas within the context of the instructions you have been given. For this reason a critique stage is essential when the first concepts are drawn up. Try not to be over-enthusiastic, and certainly not complacent, when a concept emerges after a long period of research. Instead, stand back and evaluate your ideas with a critical eye or seek the opinion of others. There is no point in embarking on detailed design work until you have reached a verdict on the concept. Ask yourself a number of questions which will help you to gauge whether the emerging design works. Does the idea for the design match your own understanding and interpretation of the market? Can you sell the idea with confidence? Would the public be able to relate easily to your concept and understand it? Is the idea original enough to stand up to close scrutiny and is it suitable for its intended task.

Experimental first stages

When a design begins it is important to find an aspect on which you can focus your attention. This project requires the created image to set a theme for the entire business, and so the designers investigate images that help achieve this. Each designer seems to be looking in a very different direction, from fine art of this century to images of women's fashions and lifestyles in the 1930s. Each route demonstrates an individual, yet valid launching point.

The methods used to compile the visual research base and to develop options are not for the client's eyes but to give the designer an overview of possible approaches. In the early stages technique should not be a major

■ **Student A**
2 The student developed flowing images relating to Isadora Duncan. She looked for colors and shapes that would be identified with the 1930s and could be applied in the creation of a house style. The miniature book is the beginning of an idea.

3 These shapes were developed from the initial idea in the miniature book. It was now possible to explore 1930s imagery more precisely using color and art deco images.

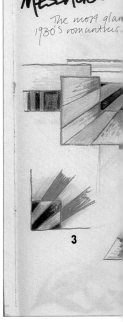
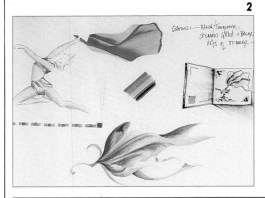
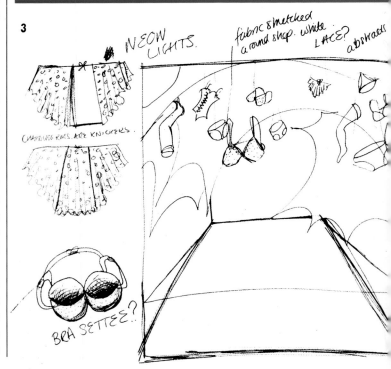

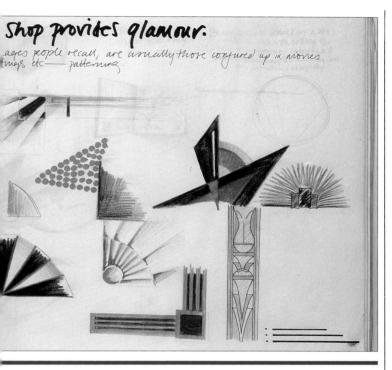

shop provides glamour.

*ages people recall, are usually those conjured up in movies
rings etc — patterning.*

■ **Student B**
3 Looking further for sculpted shapes the student became influenced by surrealist images.

■ **4** The interesting linear shapes were formed to create different objects reflecting the human form, movement, and shape.

knuckers, bras etc.

*suspended in mid air
stiffened. like people in
room in single
colour. BLACK?*

matt
*all white —
everything*

*IT WOULD MAKE THEM
MOVE AROUND*

*all white
of course
push texture
inside*

4

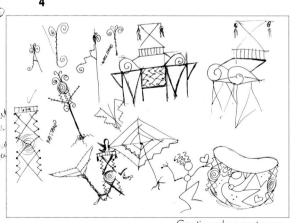

Continued on next page

consideration, and in fact the more experimental the visual approach the more variety is likely to emerge. The key to these visuals is the designer's own awareness of the possibilities they offer.

The above is not intended to minimize the importance of developing good visual sequences, and each designer should attempt to display his or her ideas with the maximum care and integrity. Good worksheets make it easier to follow the evolution of ideas. They should be seen as a diary of the development of visual information.

Putting ideas into visual form

When you have lived with your initial ideas for the time allotted to the first stage, turning over the welter of permutations in your mind, you should begin to investigate visual directions on paper. First of all, try to put down all those ideas that flash through your mind. You could create a flow chart which firmly fixes these early abstract thoughts as words on the page for further exploration.

To do this, start with the core subject – in this case lingerie. This becomes the hub from which lines can be developed, much as spokes radiate from the hub of a wheel. This process allows the most mundane thoughts to develop into bizarre or original concepts. As you can see, from the single word "underwear," Italian, classic, statues, art, classical paintings, old masters, and artists spring to mind. From these words new concepts are formed, and so the process of evolving ideas takes shape.

Another approach is to start with visual stimuli. Look through your scrapbooks and magazines for pictures that are relevant to the initial image-making. A third method is to develop ideas on separate sheets of paper. The process is similar to the wheel principle described above, but each line is formed on a separate sheet. Ultimately this approach will occur naturally at a later stage when the ideas that are valid will be further developed.

From the processes described above, pictures begin to form. The next crucial stage is a concept for the interpretation of these visual forms.

Synthesized visual information can be abstracted from found images, which can be adapted to provide new forms. You will now have to decide which information to synthesize, as this will shape your thinking as you proceed with your work.

Rarely do visual ideas emerge from a vacuum. The designer is reliant on knowledge that is best gained through familiarity with the visual arts and literature. Also useful is a broad interest in current and historical affairs. Once the research material is gathered and its elements analyzed, the craft is to extract the relevant information and model it according to the requirements of the project.

Images within a time span

Researching a project can take a lot of time. To survive in a competitive commercial world where time is costed for each piece of work, the next stage, creating client visuals, must be carried out with a deliberate, swift and confident technique. This is where the formative process of learning how to manipulate media, modeling them to give the right emphasis and sympathy to the desired image, comes into play. If you are fully aware of the qualities that different graphic applications will give your work, discovering the right visual tone should not be difficult. Here the early part of your research work will determine the speed and success of what you want to present.

Once the images begin to achieve the message you wish them to convey, and all

5

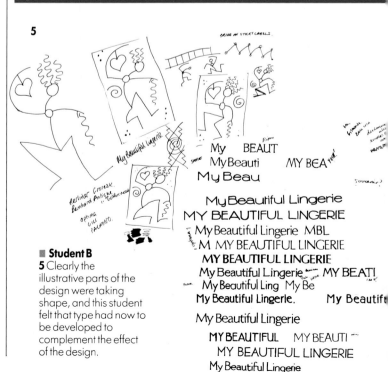

5

■ **Student B**
5 Clearly the illustrative parts of the design were taking shape, and this student felt that type had now to be developed to complement the effect of the design.

■ Student A

5 Linear forms and flowing body lines were now explored to seek out a device that would give the right 1930s styling and establish a logo.

6

27 THE SPIRES

CHIPPING

BARNET

6 A key factor in the design was choosing the right typeface to echo the 1930s theme.

7

7 The design was now taken a stage further to test its application. A major item of all corporate work is the stationery, and this was one of many early layouts.

6

My Beautiful
Lingerie

6 The type and linear illustration now combined forces. The student evaluated different type, weight, colors, and layout of shape.

MY BEAUTIFUL LINGERIE.

7

MY BEAUTIFUL

MY BEAUTIFUL

7 The linear form needed more thought and development, as it lacked visual emphasis. A thermographic approach was applied to the illustration, and some experiments were carried out using silver paint mixed with epoxy resin.

MY BEAUTIFUL
LINGERIE

Continued on next page

other routes have been eliminated through rational criticism, the creation of client visuals can start. You can now demonstrate the visual versatility of your chosen concept. However, it is no good creating a good concept and running out of energy in its application. Often, a lesser idea that offers more options is more impressive than a grander but less flexible one, and therefore more likely to succeed when shown to the client.

The client presentation

We have seen that the development of the design student's personal creativity should be tempered by the need to respond to commercial constraints. It is at the client presentation stage that it becomes obvious whether the student has really gotten to the root of the problem and is both thinking creatively and responding fully to the demands of the client. While the financial constraints of the business world usually call for cost-effective and restrained design, there is no reason why successful campaigns should not be the result of initial adventurous ideas. To be successful in the future, the student designer must be aware of the need to balance these two demands.

A key factor in selling your design to your client is how you put it across. Your display of visuals represents your shop. Consequently, if your presentation resembles a messy corner store, you will be judged by the low value you yourself seem to place on your work. Alternatively, a polished presentation offering a range of options will convey prestige and quality.

It is not enough to come up with a good graphic design idea. You are the person with a trained eye, not your client, so a good presentation must show every facet of the design, skillfully drawn and represented.

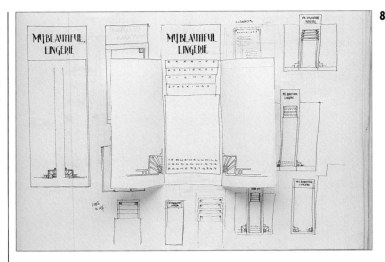

8

■ **Student A**
8 Now the components of the design had been firmly established, the opportunity for different visual applications was taken. Sheets of experimental layouts were quickly produced to assess the proportions of the design.

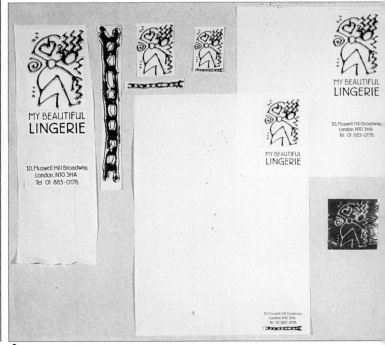

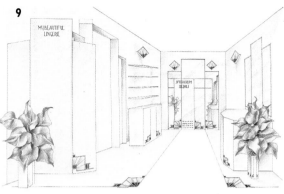

9

MY BEAUTIFUL LINGERIE

9 The final idea was then developed to show its versatility in application. Client visuals were produced to show the design in its finished form on stationery, in shop interiors, and on the components with the interior.

9 The final logo was created using a thermographic process to raise the image. The use of silver suggests luxury and adds solidity. The lightness of the typography complements the final image.

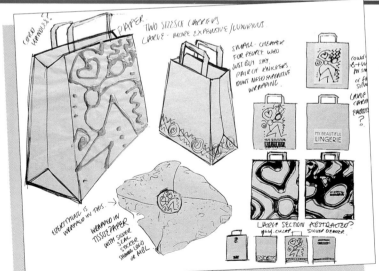

■ Student B
8 The next stage was to test the logo on a number of different stationery items.

9

MY BEAUTIFUL
LINGERIE

Critique

Among the criteria for judging the success of the work, the most important are its originality, the interpretation of the commission's requirements, the work's suitability for the intended purpose, and its application to a variety of related uses. When you have selected the work that seems to have the most potential, a further question emerges: which design works best for the product? This automatically leads to a more fundamental question: how well did the students pursue their ideas through to a finished state, and did they all show a commitment to produce an effective solution?

While the students were learning the process of design they were in fact competing for a real job. The work that was produced provided a corporate image for a real commercial business. The work that was finally chosen appears more conventional than the other two attempts, although it is evident that this student rightly paid close attention to all she discovered about her client. The appropriateness of the chosen design to its intended tasks should not be ignored. It uses forms with well-researched associations, the luxurious art deco styling giving the products the right status. This nostalgic image is a winning formula because of the strength of its associations with quality. The colors used were developed thoroughly and were well chosen for their soft, silky pastel shades. The successful work embodied every facet of the client's own feelings about the products, projecting a reassuring image of comfort and luxury by reinterpreting a retrospective theme.

The shortcomings of the other two design solutions were their more abstract concepts, which left an element of doubt in the mind of the client. Despite their originality, they presented a risk of misinterpretation which

■ Student A
The chosen design The finished print shown here clearly demonstrates the student's ability to take a concept through to a conclusion.

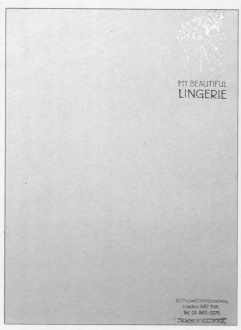

any client would be unwilling to take.

What the students have learned by hindsight from this project is that self-discipline plays a vital part in the creative process. Good ideas suffer from the lack of relentless interpretation. Perfection is possible only by continuous visualization and the rejection of unsatisfactory work. Some ideas were well developed but nevertheless fell short on the subtle process of marrying the design concept to the product. Conversely, good technique was sometimes used to disguise weak design ideas.

■ Student C

This arty solution to the assignment is fun and frivolous – an alternative approach which did not find favor with this particular client.

■ Student B
Original but unsophisticated These designs are imaginative and original but lack the subtlety and taste necessary to this type of product. Although it is perfectly acceptable as a student to pursue originality, a commercial awareness and an understanding of what the client is after must be developed for real-life commissions.

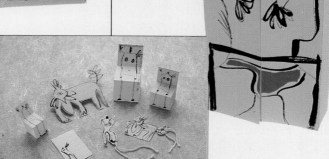

Editorial design: SEMINAR

COLIN McHENRY, Group Art Director for Centaur Publications, London.

In my role as Group Art Director at Centaur, I rely on my team of experienced art editors and copy editors for the continued success of our newspapers and magazines. I stress the word "team," because this is a key element in successful editorial design continuity. Let me explain a little about how a magazine is created.

When a new magazine is proposed the editorial staff and design staff will meet with the publisher's directors to discuss the proposal and take instructions on its further

■ **Above** This cover and inside pages from *Business* magazine are effective design solutions.

development. At this point we ask as many questions as we can, and also the Publishing Director, aware of the time that will be involved, prepares a well-thought-out brief.

The type of publication involved determines the route we take. If it is a publication that is going to be visually managed by our copy editors, then the task will be different from what is demanded by a publication with its own individual art editor. The art editor's job is to edit the visual elements in much the same way as the editor edits the words.

There are really just two

sorts of magazine I deal with: creative titles and more formal business titles. The first are overseen by the art editors, who structure each of the pages, laying out and arranging the visual and typographical material for each issue. The business titles

"The test of good design is whether the design still continues to work without the critical eye of its originator."

must have more hardworking design specifications as they are laid out by the copy editors, who are not trained designers.

The subs control the information and display it on the strength of its content. They will edit copy down and decide on the position for each article, bearing in mind that the design format and type styles are predetermined and used as a formula for each publication.

When designing the magazine, particular care needs to be taken to slot advertisements in without affecting the design. The test of good design is whether the design still continues to work without the critical eye of its originator , and for this it should be in the safe hands of a strong team.

Good magazine design does not come from complicated use of type, grids, or layout. Quite the contrary – it comes from simple, well-formulated, tight design. What do I mean by "tight" design? A simple straightforward grid of two, three, or four columns is perfectly adequate for any layout. The idea that a complex grid will assist your design only adds to the problems. It is true that you can make the page look different, but then how much more impressive it is to create new ideas using the structures that work.

It is also interesting to ask a design student to tell you how many typefaces are used in the creation of a well-respected magazine such as *Elle*. The usual response is that a number of typefaces must be used to create the varied and interesting design layouts to be seen in this publication. In this they would probably be wrong. I believe that only two typefaces are used – one for text and one for headlines, subheads, and quotes. This shows that with tight control a single typeface can offer many variations, and one face is, in fact, a whole family of weights and stylings.

My advice about layout is to consider the heading as a SHOUT! You should visually SPEAK LOUDLY about introducing text, such as subheads, cross-heads, quotation marks etc. The main text or body copy should simply TALK. This formula, if you stick to it, never fails. What it allows you to do is to think about type style and the tonal appearance of the page.

Fads and fashion
A lot is said about trying to create new styles with quirky typefaces. I believe there are good reasons why serif faces have been traditionally used by the world's leading magazine designers. Above all, they are just more readable. Some of the best typefaces were designed over 100 years ago. I can think of many, but Century and Bodoni take some beating. You may think once you put the typeface down, that is the end of it. But it is what you do then that really counts.

By nicely proportioning the leading between the lines you can change the whole feel of the typeface and so change the design of the layout. Sans-serif faces work better as headlines, but can be used to great effect in short, snappy pieces of copy, although you would be hard pressed to read an entire book set in a sans-serif face.

When I went to college no one even told me about fitting copy, but I learned a lot about making images that look good, so it was later worth the effort to study the technical side of typography, and it is all the easier when you are interested.

This awareness is what I look for in students. They should be bright, well-read, and ready to learn new things. They will have to deal with highly literate editors who will not take kindly to someone who cannot understand the content of a manuscript or interpret a commission. This knowledge should be wide ranging – the more general it is, the better.

Finally, I believe students should always apply for the best jobs going. If you start on a quality title you will soon move up the scale and the work will become even more absorbing and challenging.

I went into magazines almost as an extension of my childhood hobby of collecting and compiling scrapbooks. My main interest was the Beatles and I enjoyed cutting out pictures and arranging them on a page. The idea that some pages worked and some did not I found really appealing.

A good page layout should indicate clearly where the piece starts and where it finishes and it should encourage the reader to read. It is no good making each page of a magazine look totally different. This was a fashion in the early 1980s, with magazines such as *The Face*, although if you analyze this I think you will see an underlying tight grid, and today's

"A good page layout should indicate clearly where the piece starts and where it finishes."

publication has become even more formal. However, because the design worked to begin with, the tightening up of spreads has been achieved, at the same time while retaining the original concept of the page layouts.

I emphasize the disadvantage of making each spread different because my experience tells me that the magazine as a whole works better if you allow only those pages that can accommodate special design to be given special treatment. If every page was forced to do something different you would end up with a confusing and messy publication. It is better to have a smooth flow of consistent page layouts, occasionally broken by some difference in the design because of, say, an illustration or photograph or a special heading or subhead.

Interpreting ideas

Magazines are not just about typography and layout – they are also very much about illustration and photography. In previous jobs I discovered how important illustration was by working at *Radio Times*, and later how important photography was while Art Editor at *Good Housekeeping*. As a magazine designer, you are required to commission illustration. This means you must acquire many skills. The first is the ability to interpret a manuscript. You need to be able to

read it, understand it, and get some visual ideas from it.

Where do the illustration ideas come from? It is unlikely you will be a trained illustrator as well as a designer. What you need to do is start collecting references from all the publications you look at. It is no good just looking through the yearbooks or at advertisements placed by agents in the illustration contact books. They will only show you the work of established illustrators and not the new talent. Once you have read the text and decided on the theme of an illustration from all your own references, it is a delight to sit down and discuss the page with your illustrator. You must decide what proportions the image will have on the page, whether the copy will run around it, or whether it will occupy its own space. Will the edges of the illustration be left ragged or be cropped, and will it bleed off the page? That is only the beginning. The next consideration is the color. Will the illustration be printed in full color, in flat solid colors, in hints or tints? Or in black and white with added tones? What I find

most exciting is to see the final piece which interprets beautifully all of the initial thoughts and ideas.

Using photography creatively

Photography gives the magazine designer another opportunity for experimentation. I have heard people say that the photographs they have found or have been supplied with for a spread have no design potential. But this is rarely true, and if you think of a single photograph as containing the potential for a range of images, then the opportunities are immense. I mean by this that you need to find the right composition within the image.

Say you are working with a single portrait and you wish to extract more than one picture from this single image. By cropping out sections, for

example the eyes, you can create a powerful image. Perhaps by cutting the portrait very close in you will turn a dry-looking image into something quite punchy. This is the basic use of photography on a magazine. The work gets much more exciting when you art-direct your own photographs.

You do not need to know much about the technical side of photography to art-direct – the photographer does all that. What you do need to know is how the photographic studio set-up works. You can only really learn this by standing in on photographic shoots and use this knowledge when setting up your own photo session. As with illustrators, you need to be familiar with the choice of photographers available and the variety of current styles.

■ **Above** *Good Housekeeping* is known for its use of stylish photography and layouts.

Editorial design: INTRODUCTION

New magazines, books, and other publications appear on the newsstands and in book stores, and supermarkets every day of the year. For this specialized area of design the graphic designer needs to be particularly aware of what he is creating. Magazines and books are three-dimensional products, and their creation raises important questions. Who will purchase the product? What are their interests, social awareness, income levels? In short, what is the nature of the potential readership?

In designing a new publication, or revamping an existing one, you are targeting a readership pinpointed by detailed research. It is therefore logical to analyze the visual approach used in other publications aimed at a similar target. But do not be misled by the choice of images in publications that are losing sales or are going out of fashion. Remember that all sectors of the market, from children to sophisticated adults, like to see some change and expect some progression in the images they view. But, as with corporate designs, once a publication is designed its look is usually retained for several years.

Styling the publication

The structure of a book or magazine can be broken down into two elements: the front cover and the internal matter. The front cover has two functions. It has to sell the general concept of the publication at the point-of-sale and to reflect, through its design, the intellectual level of the editorial content.

The cover of a magazine is one of the main means of promoting sales, and it is the consistency and appeal of its design that maintain its readership and attract new readers. The cover of a book must first promote the author's work in a style and manner that complements the content.

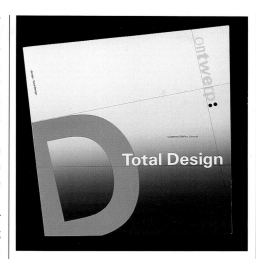

Secondly, as a piece of packaging it must perform the function of a point-of-sale display. This means that it must sell itself directly from the shelf.

Magazines are rarely left to evolve from the ideas of a single designer, but are highly influenced by expert marketing advice and corporate styling. A substantial financial investment is made when a new national magazine is launched. It is the responsibility of the designer to gain a full understanding of both the marketing strategy and the visual tone which will attract the projected readership.

■ **Inspirational designs**
These progressive designs are distinguished by their effective use of typography and grid .

■ Use the grid as a basis for experimentation.
■ Keep it simple to allow creative flexibility.
■ Work in miniature, as this gives you less work in realizing your layouts.
■ Try out different proportions and shapes for your pictures.
■ Look at the columns of type as tonal areas.
■ Try punctuating these tonal areas with heavier forms representing headings and subheadings.
■ Experiment extensively with these elements to discover the variations that can be created.

Editorial design: LAYOUT DESIGN

The layout of a magazine or book will first be conditioned by its format. Non-standard paper sizes are, of course, much more costly than standard ones. That said, an unusual format does set the publication apart from its neighbors on the bookstand. Magazines that are larger than average are more flexible, enabling you to use grids more creatively. And yet a pocket-sized publication can also be unusual in appearance, exploiting the precision which is characteristic of small formats. A great deal depends on the editorial content and how it needs to be presented to the reader.

Once you have decided on the format, you must consider a formula for your design. The two major aspects of design that test your subtlety in this area are the grid, used to give a consistent structure to each page, and the typographic style, with its particular tonal quality.

Editorial design offers a creative platform for the designer with a passion for combining type and image. It brings together particular attention to typographic effects and the creative use of illustration and photography that complement the type.

Even with the most conventional job – a trade publication, for example – there are formulas that give an inventiveness to a design or layout. A publication has a predetermined grid, usually of three or four columns. These columns carry the type and are a practical vehicle for the typesetter to follow on every page or edition. With modern desktop publishing systems the grid is a key element in the design structure. If the grid has been well thought out it will allow the information to be displayed with ease and continuity.

By using the grid as the formal base to the work you can then begin to move beyond its boundaries. You can create shapes that

LAYOUT DESIGN ASSIGNMENT

Set up a simple three- or four-column grid for a trade magazine called *On Site*. The columns for this grid should be equally spaced with a small margin between the columns. You should then decide on the space at the head and foot of the page as well as the outer edge and the gutters. This space should be measured in picas or millimeters or using the Didot system.

Design requirements
Once you have created your grid, this will form the basis for you to create alternative layout designs. The spreads should include pictures and invented headings to give a sense of reality to the project. How you treat the pictures is left to you.

Technical requirements
Produce a number of "thumbnails" (miniature layouts) exhausting the possibilities of your pictures and type combined. Using one of the layout ideas, develop it into a presentation visual. This must be a double-page spread.

■ **Photo references**
Photographs supplied for magazine layouts may form the basis for illustrations or may be used in part and displayed in an attractive way. Are these images good enough and sharp enough? If not, they can be used as reference for illustrations.

■ Grid layouts Here, the student has decided on a four-column grid, and thumbnail sketches have been produced to get an idea of how image and type will fall on the page. At this stage of the work not enough consideration has been given to margins and gutters; white space should be left around the text throughout the design, allowing for the fact that the pages will eventually be trimmed.

challenge the structure itself. The tonal effect of type can be harnessed to keep the design orderly and flowing. Objects can be placed on the surface, either as photographs or illustrations, and many techniques can be applied to alternative layout arrangements. Imagine a photograph of a single object with no background – overlaid with the structure of the grid. This could be the size of a full page. You would discover that the object leaves areas of the grid that do not obscure it. These areas can be used for columns of text, and this creates an almost three-dimensional effect in which the copy appears to float above and around the object.

Similarly, you can look at photographs or illustrations as objects and draw around their shapes. These shapes can then be used to break the columns, creating an exciting visual arrangement. Photographs can be converted into illustrations, and by tracing these using colored pencils or markers you can transform ordinary, everyday objects into illustrations with visual appeal.

Basic lessons

The first learning process in understanding layout comes with the confidence and excitement of discovering how to manipulate text and images into various new forms. An interplay of formal and informal shapes can be shifted around the space to create endless combinations.

To find the best solution for a particular layout, experiment with all the elements. By enlarging and reducing illustrations or photographs, and cropping these to extract the best images, you will make the layout convey different moods. The typography needs the same scrutiny, and in choosing the typeface you need to select an image that complements the other elements. Look at the spaces between the lines and see how these

Editorial design: PAGE LAYOUT

affect the appearance. Changing the interlinear spacing can have as marked an effect on the look of a block of type as changing type size or line length.

The project commissions described in this section of the book offer an ideal platform for adventurous layout and image manipulation.

You will see how type is structured by the use of grids. You will also learn about the different methods used for indicating type in a layout and how photocopies can be cut and used to give an idea of how much space the type will occupy. You can see how pictures can be constructed and overlaid and converted into a single color or made into a drawing. Cropping pictures is also discussed. You will discover that there are similarities between collage and layout, since most of the elements can be represented as cut-out shapes within a design space.

The book layouts (pages 148-153) will show you how the sense of the subject can dictate the styling of a page, for the subject matter must be expressed in a complementary way. A single page or a double-page spread must not be considered in isolation, and by studying the various approaches in the assignments in this section you will see how the student designer can set a theme that creates a flow of pages.

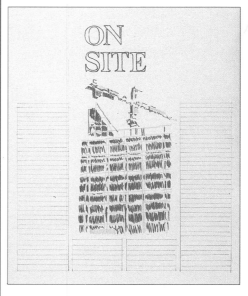

■ **Working larger** The next stage after thumbnail sketches (above) is to test the idea on a larger scale — this does not need to be to the finished size.

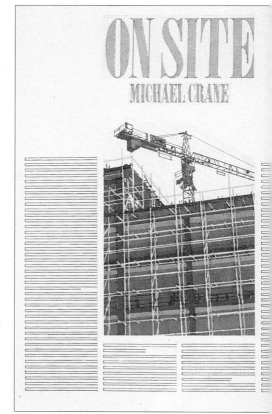

■ **Final layout** The left-hand page is beginning to come together (right); the formal arrangement of the type could be punctuated with some devices. The right-hand page, which departs from the grid, is both complex to produce typographically and ineffective visually. However, the presentation of the work is competent and achieves a commercially acceptable quality.

Critique

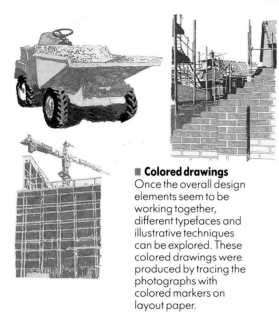

■ **Colored drawings**
Once the overall design elements seem to be working together, different typefaces and illustrative techniques can be explored. These colored drawings were produced by tracing the photographs with colored markers on layout paper.

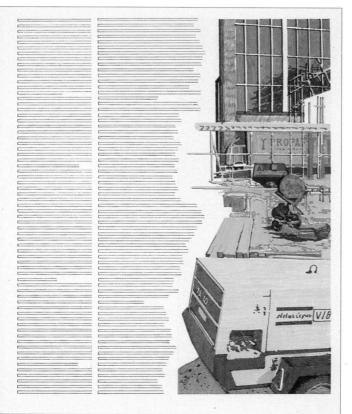

The final layout for this *On Site* double-page spread uses a four-column grid. The outer margins are kept tight, as are the head and foot of the page. The central gutter is wider than any of these margins – a basic fault in the first stage of the design. The effect of this wide gutter is to make the pages appear separate when they should be unified. The gutter is usually the same overall measure as the outer margin because, once bound, the gutter width is reduced. To compensate for this, the visual should deliberately be made to look tighter. The four-column grid enables you to be flexible. The two pairs of columns can also be combined to make two wide columns.

The left-hand page with the heading creates a spacious feeling. Aligning the illustration with the heading makes an interesting compositional layout. The four columns of text that run around the picture have been indicated in double lines, and although they give a nice tonal balance they lack typographic styling. To achieve a more interesting effect with the type, indents should be allowed for paragraph breaks, with the possible inclusion of featured enlarged capital letters and subheadings.

The right-hand page features interesting visualizations created from photographic references, although the typography fails to work successfully. The main factor is the sudden departure from the grid by the type. The sudden imbalance of column width strikes a discordant note.

Understandably, the student wished to create a pattern with the type that runs around the illustration. To make this work he could have moved the illustration more to the left, allowing the text to be set to its normal column width and offering the possibility of the illustration breaking into the column of type in just one or two places.

Editorial design: MAGAZINES

Let's now turn our attention to magazines on specific subjects such as architecture or engineering, dressmaking or recruitment, and look at how the designer would go about the research, visualizing, and planning of the cover, and all the component parts of a new publication, aimed at a particular type of reader, be it professional, enthusiast, or hobbyist.

When tackling a commission to design a magazine, the first things you have to ask yourself are: who are the readers of the proposed publication likely to be, and what are their interests beyond the subject of the magazine itself?

As a starting point, make a brief assessment of the range of magazines already available for a similar readership. You may have to search in major public libraries and specialist bookstores and in foreign embassies or trade centers.

Researching the market

Once you have a wide selection of relevant publications, choose a number of articles to read about different topics, and assess their tone and the level they aim for. Picture the kind of person reading this material. It is well known that effective advertising is carefully targeted, so by assessing the tone of the advertising in general, you will automatically be tapping into the research already done by advertising agencies. For example, the recruitment section will clearly indicate the type of readership at which the magazine is aimed. Other forms of advertising will indicate lifestyles, hobbies, and interests.

Once you have formed an idea of the target audience, you need to assess the visual success of the individual contents. Look at the way typography is used and the style of the typefaces; think about their relevance and effectiveness. Look for the underlying struc-

NEW MAGAZINE ASSIGNMENT

To design a magazine entitled *Architecture*, aimed at an international market. Because of the ever-widening interest in architecture, the magazine you are going to create needs to inform not only the professional architect but also a broader, non-expert readership. The function of the magazine is to review modern architecture throughout the world. The reviews will cover buildings ranging from the massive Pompidou Centre in Paris or developments in London's Docklands to small, innovative projects. There will also be extensive coverage of architecture from the past and features on the latest street furniture and related subject material.

Design requirements
The masthead needs to be designed to set a house style. You have to produce a front cover accommodating the masthead; the contents page; a news review double-page spread; a three-page major feature that starts on a double-page spread.

Technical requirements
This magazine is published monthly. Full color is used throughout. There is no restriction on the format, although basic grids should be made available to assist the styling of future issues. Specify type style and house typefaces.

■ **Student A**
References First, the designer looks at the marketplace, investigating all types of magazine design and their styling. It is clear that the student has already aimed his magazine concept at a sophisticated audience.

■ **Student B**
Masthead roughs
Thorough research in the form of notes and sketches acts as a springboard for visual ideas. The theme of classical linked to modern gives an underlying unity to these initial roughs. The "A" is evolving as a classical architectural form.

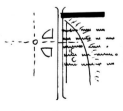

138

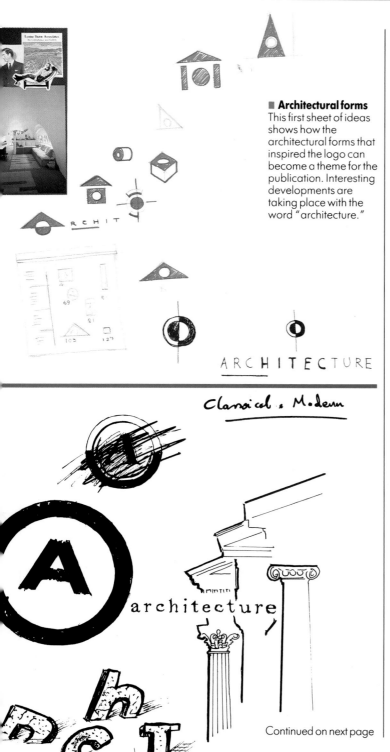

■ **Architectural forms**
This first sheet of ideas shows how the architectural forms that inspired the logo can become a theme for the publication. Interesting developments are taking place with the word "architecture."

ARCHITECTURE

Classical & Modern

architecture

Continued on next page

ture used for creating and styling the assembled pages. What sort of formula, such as a grid, holds the information in place?

The grid

Grid size and the number of column divisions are influenced by the format of the publication, and therefore grid shape and size of page are considered together. The larger the format the greater the scope for wide outer and inner margins and the greater the number of column divisions. It is normally accepted that a readable length of line would consist of 50-70 type characters, 70 being the maximum advisable in any line of continuous prose.

The simplest form of grid is a single column. This can be subdivided into smaller columns, creating a more flexible arrangement. Remember that the divisions of the grid, namely the columns, should be separated equally for consistent typesetting. The more complex your grid, the more flexibility it allows for design. Most magazine work contains different types of information and illustrative displays. There are short passages of text, such as news items, longer articles, advertisements, illustrations from postage-stamp size to those that fill a double-page spread, and captions, sidebars, headings, subheadings, and many other typographical devices to consider.

Clearly the most influential aspect of a page is how each area is used tonally within the available space. Look for the shapes the type creates on the page. Look at this in both negative and positive form, considering the white areas (the "negative shapes") as a design element in themselves. By moving around the page blocks of gray or black areas of type, cut to different column lengths, you can invent a variety of layouts. This is just one aspect of the layout that will help you understand how to create moods and tension within the design. Naturally, a single page should not be considered in isolation, and double-page spreads must work harmoniously, both pages being considered together as an integral design.

Once a system has been devised which accommodates all the elements in their required proportion, this becomes the model to be followed throughout the publication. The column widths need not be uniform, but they should conform to the page grid that underlies each page layout. However, breaking out of the grid is a natural progression for all adventurous designers. In searching for an unusual or lively spread you may feel tempted to experiment, for while uniformity can be attractive, too much of it makes the design dull. You need to strike a balance between those pages that are formal in approach and those that break the mold. Too many busy layouts within one publication will create an overworked and cluttered look.

Looking at typefaces

Typefaces are subject to fashion, although for editorial layout the most popular and readable typefaces remain those in the serif ranges. The design of serif typefaces has changed throughout the centuries, providing an abundance of type styles from which to choose.

The refinement of printed information and the ever-increasing number of competitive publications have created a situation in which designed typefaces have been specially cut for new publications and new ideas about image-making have developed to give the printed word a different visual appeal. Type design and type production houses are major businesses which compete vigorously for the designer's custom. They supply catalogues for the designer and you as a student

■ **Student A**
Thumbnail sketches The next consideration is page format (right). This early sketch of the front cover starts to explore layout and how images and type can be arranged within the space to give a feeling of luxury.

■ **Flexible grid**
Following the theme of the front cover, the inside pages echo the luxury of space with a flexible grid of three and two columns. The squares represent picture positions and graphic devices between copy, breaking up the tone of the gray.

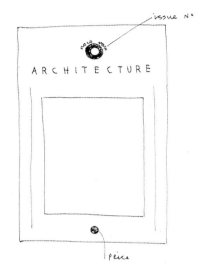

■ **Student B**
Thumbnail sketches These initial drawings (above right) explore possible solutions for the front cover of the magazine. Two ideas are unfolding, utilizing different decal devices for the masthead and dramatically contrasting pictures.

■ **Overlapping grid** The inside pages shown here as thumbnails (right) investigate the possibility of overlapping grids, with a page division of three columns, overlaid with one central column. The logo acts as a unifying device.

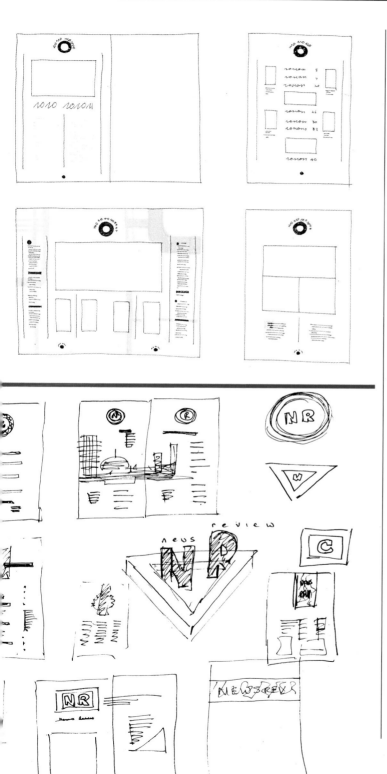

designer, should acquire as many of these as possible so that you can compare the typeface selection and sample setting they offer. Note that these businesses hold only a selection of typefaces, not every face that has been created.

The only way to assess the effects created by these typefaces is to seek out sample setting that will show you how specific types look when made up into columns. It is not good enough just to select your type from the typeface catalogues, however extensive, as you need to see it made up to assess its readability and the styling it conveys. You should also consider type for its tonal quality on the page and try differing weights of the same face or compatible contrasting typefaces in the styling of the page. Remember that a typeface must be readable as well as attractive on the page.

It is also important to assess the historical relevance of the type to the subject matter, bearing in mind that many typefaces of the 20th century were designed specifically to break tradition and change the visual art of typographic layout. For example, it would be impossible to set body text in a typeface such as Bifur. However, if you wanted to create a heading evocative of art deco, this face could be suitable. Some faces are timeless – Bembo and Bodoni, for example – and although their use fluctuates, they will always remain popular for their delicate lines and readability.

The work of the Constructivist movement, and especially that of El Lissitzky, shaped a new European concept of type layout design. This influence, along with that of the Parisian *Mise en Page* and the work of Theo van Doesburg, helped to structure the distinctive new generation of sans-serif typefaces of the 20th century. *Mise en Page* (Page Layout) was created by a Parisian printer, A.

Tolmer, to combine art and layout in a single book and has acted as an inspiration since its publication in 1931. Van Doesburg's magazine *De Stijl* became an inspirational force setting trends in layout design that were pursued later in the Bauhaus.

■ **Mise en Page** Page layout designed by

A. Tolmer from his book *Mise en Page* (1931).

There is no pattern book for the right styling, for you are always trying to find the most creative solution and possibly the most visually different spread. Remember, it is not by accident that serif typefaces are used for most publications. Times, Century, Bembo and others, have long been used for designs where there is an overwhelming amount of text. The reason is that these faces are the most readable.

The design takes shape

Now that you have completed the considerable initial research, some visual forms will have come to mind. These will constitute the initial roughs. You may wish to use them as a point of departure for greater development of individual sections of the magazine. For example, you may want to formalize the way typography and illustration control the inside pages. You may want to let the design be influenced by the subject matter of the magazine.

Photographs can be diffused, montaged, or reconstructed in various forms in the search for a graphic formula for your design.

■ **Student A**
Working up a visual
Once an idea has come to mind, a visual will firmly establish how potentially successful the idea might be. The student has been selective in the visual information that has been displayed, giving subtle emphasis to the HITEC feature. Existing photographs for collage and styling were found to put this visual together

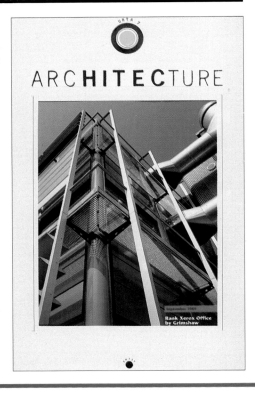

■ **Student B**
Alternative visuals The earlier roughs were now developed into visuals for further discussion. The circular motif emerged as the most popular device; type and layout have been used sympathetically with the found photographic material. The choice still remained as to which of these images was most suitable for this publication.

Type as layout Using found type images, the student was able to begin thinking about typefaces in the context of the design.

■ **Developing the layout** Once the structure and type styles were established they were then included in a mock-up of the contents page. Again, collage was used for type and pictures.

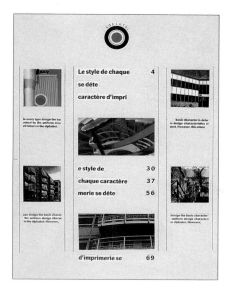

Le style de chaque	4
se déte	
caractère d'impri	

e style de	30
chaque caractère	37
merie se déte	56

| d'imprimerie se | 69 |

Type and layout The page layouts investigate the use of type set to an asymmetric formula, and complemented by spacious areas of white. The type creates interesting tonal patterns within the design space.

between

function

and

rhetoric.

The easiest way to hit on the right approach is to start drawing out your ideas as thumbnails but with the same proportions as the shapes you plan to use full size.

Photographs and illustrations, and heavy and light lines depicting tonal effects of type, can quickly be rendered with thick and thin markers. Shapes and devices can be invented and stress can be placed on the way space affects the layout. Once you feel more confident about the emerging layout, you can start to produce larger, quarter-scale visuals. Try to be objective about your ideas, as preconceptions of how a design should appear can hamper creativity. You must be highly critical and brave enough to discard ideas at any stage.

It may be best to work on the inside pages first, as this will help you formulate concepts for the most testing piece of this design project: the front cover. This part of the task is a great challenge to all designers, for a precise and yet eye-catching arrangement of the elements is called for. Your choice of typefaces for the cover should reflect the structure, visual theme, and the all-important contents of the publication. This is best done by sketching the cover full size in pencil, and creating alternatives from the original thumbnail sketches. You can also photocopy the graphic elements at different sizes in order to experiment with alternative layouts.

The next stage of your visual is to create some dummy pages. These can be made full size and need only be worked up roughly to give a full impression of the actual design. They can be refined when minor problems have been resolved. The photocopier, again, is a versatile tool for altering the size and density of type when constructing text blocks or single lines such as headings, or cover lines.

■ Student A
Coordinating the layouts

The grid and column measure have now been refined. The outer rule surrounding the columns of text has set a style to follow on all the spreads. Drop capitals have been used, and the typography has set an appropriate tone. The circular device has now been color-coded to identify separate sections of the magazine. Color photographs have been integrated into black-and-white illustrations, and strong colors have been used to link with the heading above.

■ Student B
Developing layout style

The tonal use of type has created illustrative patterns, making each layout unified but very individual in style. Texture and tone are the central theme running throughout the pages, with each spread designed individually on its own merit. However, there seems to be no regular structure for text to follow.

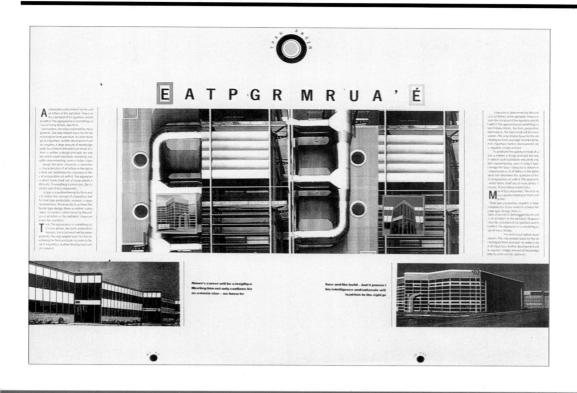

E A T P G R M R U A ' É

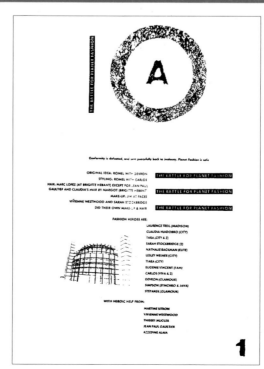

THE BATTLE FOR PLANET FASHION

Conformity is defeated, and sent peacefully back to jealousy. Planet Fashion is safe

ORIGINAL IDEA: ROMEL WITH DEVRON
STYLING: ROMEL WITH CARLOS
THE BATTLE FOR PLANET FASHION
HAIR: MARC LOPEZ (AT BRIGITTE HEBANT) EXCEPT FOR JEAN PAUL
GAULTIER AND CLAUDIA'S HAIR BY MARGOT (BRIGITTE HEBANT)
MAKE-UP: JIM AT FACES
THE BATTLE FOR PLANET FASHION
VIVIENNE WESTWOOD AND SARAH STOCKBRIDGE
DID THEIR OWN MAKE-UP & HAIR
THE BATTLE FOR PLANET FASHION

FASHION HEROES ARE:

LAURENCE TREIL (MADISON)
CLAUDIA HUIDOBRO (CITY)
TARA (CITY & Z)
SARAH STOCKBRIDGE (Z)
NATHALIE BACCHNAN (ELITE)
LESLEY WEINER (CITY)
TIARA (CITY)
EUGENIE VINCENT (FAM)
CARLOS (VIVA & Z)
DEVRON (GLAMOUR)
SIMPSON (SYNCHRO & JAVA)
STEPANEK (GLAMOUR)

WITH HEROIC HELP FROM:

MARTINE SITBON
VIVIENNE WESTWOOD
THIERRY MUGLER
JEAN PAUL GAULTIER
AZZEDINE ALAIA

1

T I P S

■ Research the market by seeking out influential publications, particularly from other countries.
■ Examine the structure of these publications and note how their grids work.
■ Investigate the visual effects created by different styles of typography.
■ Don't be afraid to mix typefaces in unusual combinations.
■ Try different column widths and exploit space as a feature of the publication.
■ Research examples of past and modern architecture.

Critique

Each of the solutions to this project offers an interesting individual route. Remember that this magazine is aimed at a sophisticated international audience. Therefore as a piece of graphic design it must intelligently and sympathetically reflect late-20th century thinking on architecture. It must also appear sufficiently enticing to attract, firstly, a very aware audience and, secondly, new readers venturing into this field.

Each of the three solutions seen here exhibits great potential for the use of a spacious and unusual format. The square-format version uses typography framed with extravagant margins and punctuated by an inventive use of folio numbers. It makes good use of this framing device, in which the text is set on a two-column grid with another overlay of a three-column grid, giving a geometric, bull's-eye effect to the pages. The central copy lifts itself from the surrounding text by subtle use of varying weights of type. Bold headings and a block sans-serif typeface give a roof-like structure to the pages.

The design of the pages echoes modern architecture, in that it is spacious and has the occasional hint of color. The pages work, but possibly not for this project. The feeling conveyed is more in keeping with that of a corporate brochure, and it is not sufficiently flexible to accommodate the variety of content found in a monthly magazine. Also, the front cover appears to do less than is necessary to establish a definitive image for the launch of a long-term, international title. Although excellent in concept, the design requires development to successfully fulfil the commission.

Historical approach

The second design offers a more historical approach. The pages luxuriate in open space with graphic devices which depict texture that echoes building materials, and rely heavily on layouts that are inspired by and sympathetic to Constructivist principles. The playing down of color is a strong visual feature, and hints and tints are used to soften the mechanical structures. The red circle used on the contents page pinpoints that space, announcing its importance, and links it to the circle on the cover. The decal used as a graphic identity, although attractive, over-powers some of the more important pictorial matter. The general feeling is that while the graphics are highly inventive, they detract somewhat from the editorial and pictorial content. Although extremely stylish, this solution would quickly become dated unless the design progressed with each issue.

The third concept offers a slightly more conventional approach. The format, again of generous proportions, allows flexible layouts but does not detract from the essential purpose of the publication. The illustrations depict examples of architecture in an un-embellished but thoughtfully cropped array of images. The text is displayed in readable blocks of type, and appropriate emphasis has been placed on the link between image and words.

The simple but effective title inventively splits the word with two weights of type, distinguishing "HITEC" from "ARCHITEC-TURE". This gives the magazine title another dimension which differentiates it from potential competition. The spot-color device links the front cover to the feature article, both with the yellow circle and the cover picture: a clear example of front cover being used to express content. This color coding from blue to red is used simply but effectively to divide the magazine's contents. Although this concept, too, could be developed further, it is the most effective answer to the problems set by the brief.

■ **Student A Finished layouts** The student has used existing photography in an inventive and appropriate manner. The introduction of black and white punctuated with the minimum of color makes the front cover (right) and inside spread (far right) look striking and modern.

Margins This contents page (above) was designed to establish an ongoing formula which would work consistently. Although the outer columns, used as visual features, could be less overpowering, this arrangement has established an original way of highlighting visual features to be found in the publication.

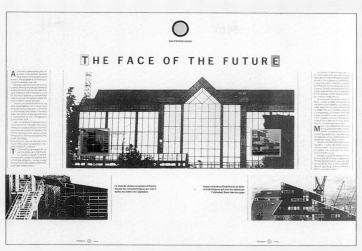

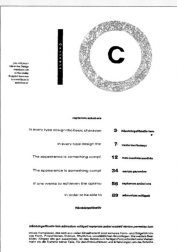

■ **Student B**
Finished layouts The visuals demonstrate technical competence and a stylish use of minimal color. The masthead has evolved to create a free shape for the title, and the layout of this cover is retained on the contents page. Although the spreads demonstrate an understanding of the use of space, this solution would demand too much additional input on individual pages to make it commercially viable.

■ **Student C**
Finished layouts This square shape is an attractive space within which to design and offers an unusual magazine format. The contents page (right) stylishly sets the theme for following spreads, although the design feels more suited to a brochure. The front cover (above right) uses the repeat pattern in a way that may be difficult to follow in further issues.

Editorial design: BOOKS

Book publishing has always provided great opportunities for the designer, and design in this field covers a vast range, from simple non-pictorial paperbacks to luxury art books. So many books are available today that each has to be well designed if it is going to compete successfully for sales.

Unlike those of most magazines, book designs can be highly complex, or quite simple, as the book itself is a single product retaining its own individual image. It is also controlled from cover to cover by the designer who initiated the design idea, so that it allows great innovation and experimentation. Layout ideas can be exploited to the full in books, although because the editorial content is still the reason for the book's existence, the way the written word is displayed must be the prime consideration in the design.

The joy inherent in designing books is that you can get involved in every facet of graphic expression. In this work you can consider carefully the qualities and influences of different papers. You can see how illustration can be manipulated and photographs taken to complement whatever image or idea the words convey. Typography can be used to set a visual tone, making the book look classic, modern, sophisticated, or restrained. Finally, the layouts, although underpinned with a book grid, can be as flexible as the job allows.

The designer also controls how the book is printed. He or she is able to lighten a picture, convert black to a color, use spot color, print black and white pictures as duotones, and use many other techniques and tricks.

Naturally, most publishers have their own ideas of how a book should look, but many are eager to try out new ways of presenting their products.

BOOK DESIGN ASSIGNMENT

There is no better way to find out about layout than by pursuing your own visual interests and making spreads of the visual material you have collected over the years. For this project think about how you would like to display these personal images.

Design requirements
Create a book as a package. It will need to be bound, with a front and back cover. It can also have a container or loose sleeve or some other device. Show the inside of the cover and the first page, using some graphic device. Show the half-title and title page and create up to five or six layouts demonstrating how the actual content is to be displayed.

Technical requirements
The book's size is to be realistic, but the shape is your decision. The number of pages should be between 144 and 200. Full color can be used if needed.

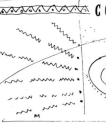

■ **Rough layouts** The first task is to get a feeling for the way space is going to be used. These early roughs investigate the different approaches to type, illustration, and layout within the space. Even at this early stage the shape and format seem to favor a square. Illustrative influences can also be seen on this sheet.

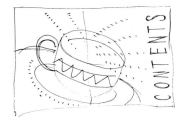

■ Type trials The only way to establish different type styles is to render them. The typefaces selected here (Bodoni, Caslon, and Century) are all traditional in feeling.

■ Layout with illustration The combination of letter-spaced type, colour and visual forms the next stage of the design. The use of space, the type of illustration, the manipulation and selection of typeface should come together as a unit in these test pieces.

CONTENTS

CONTENTS

CONTENTS

CONTENTS

CONTENTS

CONTENTS

CONTENTS

CONTENTS

■ **The right layout** The design has moved forward to incorporate the essence of the book – the teapot and cup – as an illustrative motif. The double page spread has now been planned out, and the flowing lines of the illustration work well with the subject.

here is a

■ **Old illustrations** Historical nautical engravings lend an authentic flavor to the page layouts.

■ Cut and shaped type

The theme of flowing shapes is followed through even in the typography. Letter forms can be shaped around a drawn line, either manually by

a deal of poetry & fine sentiment in a chest of tea

cutting the type and carefully positioning it to follow the desired shape, or by means of a computer program.

Countries of Origin

■ Photocopies

Maps of the world with a compass rose have been overlaid by photocopying onto tracing paper to combine the images in a collage.

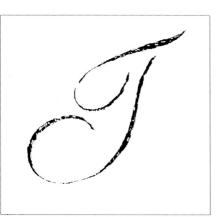

■ Making up the pages

The title page made use of a "T" which was transferred lightly on to the page by means of a linoleum cut. The speckled effect on the finished pages was used to suggest tea leaves.

Critique : BOOK DESIGN

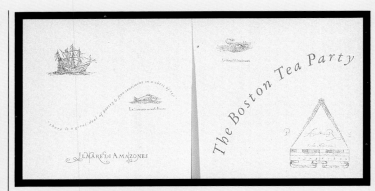

Both of these books have been created with sensitivity and care. There is no better task than designing around something to which you are truly committed.

The "T" book

The first project takes the subject of tea and explores this ancient drink with historical imagery and refined typography. The student has reinstated tea to its former historic position of importance by choosing typefaces that complement the found images, such as the woodcut illustration of compass roses, old maps, and drawings linked with the shipping of tea. Each layout delicately explores the shapes and forms of the square format of the page. This shape is good for expressive design ideas, since the geometry of the page allows for unusual layouts. It is particularly refreshing to see type used as an illustrative element in which shapes are formed out of the type itself.

What makes this book special is the way the idea of tea has been linked to the quality of paper used in the design. The speckled effect you can detect on the title page imitates the fine grain of tea leaves. In fact the student created a package to contain the book and allowed aromatic tea leaves to be included in it. This takes the concept of a tea book into a new dimension, as the grains of tea are caught between the pages and their aroma pervades the book. The front cover, simple in its approach, pinpoints a large italic serif "T" which immediately tells the reader what the book is about.

The most important aspect of this book for you to consider is the quality of papers and how they express a feeling of delicate texture. This is in keeping with the classic illustrations and typography.

■ **Finished pages** The finished pages (above) have been created by photocopying the made-up pages onto handmade paper, which gives the finished work a luxurious, quality.

■ **A complete package** The book has been bound in handmade paper with an embossed center panel carrying the title (right); it has a stiff outer casing. To enhance the effect further, loose tea leaves were placed between the pages to give the book an aroma of tea.

■ **Front cover** The second design features the history of boxing and maximizes the use of black and white illustration and space. The introduction of red is intended to represent the brutal nature of the sport. The type uses the circle and reads both clockwise and counter-clockwise.

■ **Inside the book**
Black-and-white photocopies have been diffused with tracing paper to soften the image; contrasting-colored photocopies are heavily tinted in red.

The Fight Game

The second of these books, covering the history of boxing, shows you how different the styling of a page can be. The methods used to create the page layouts rely on modern photocopying techniques. Old photographs have been tonally controlled by reducing the amount of black. Tints of color have been added to some of the pictures, with hints of ink wash. Color photocopies have also been dropped into place alongside the black and white photographs. There is a predominant and deliberate emphasis on the color red.

The use of sans-serif typefaces, punctu-ated with serif feature capitals, gives the page a stylish, modern appearance. The grid used for this book is very flexible. The widths of type columns for the running copy are consistent but have no set position on the page, although there are specific require-ments concerning margins and gutters. The pages are set up for their visual relationships of picture to text. The structures that hold most of the pages together are the large pictures that bleed off the pages, and the rest of the information is pivoted around these. The contents page departs from this, using a wide central column, while the foreword reflects the pictorial spreads.

TIPS

■ Make sure you have an interesting collection of items to display.
■ These can be three-dimensional objects,· antique items, modern images, postcards, etc.
■ Devise a logical display for your material.
■ A contents page may help with chapters or otherwise subdividing the areas of the book.
■ Imagine what the balance will be between the written word and the visual content.
■ Try out some typefaces that are sympathetic to the subject.
■ Always make thumbnail sketches before progressing to a larger scale.

Packaging: SEMINAR

PETER WINDETT, Peter Windett and Associates, Design Consultants, London.

I have worked my way up through the design business. I started at Westerham Press in 1963 where I became interested in typography, and I subsequently took up evening classes at the London College of Printing. In 1966 I was a junior designer on *Vogue*, and by 1968 I had moved to the design practice of Stratton and Wolsey. After three years as an art director, I decided to set up my own design consultancy in 1971.

Three quarters of my work is now packaging, although I never intended this to become the most significant area. In fact, quite by accident in the early 1970s, I found myself the only designer among six illustrators. This coincided with the formation of Crabtree and Evelyn, which is now our major client. I recognized at an early stage that it was important to give their range of products a timeless quality, and this could be achieved only by use of illustration. Attempts to use photography have appeared from time to

time, but the medium cannot be manipulated in the same evocative way as drawings or illustrations, where you can draw plants from nature even when they are normally out of season and add or exclude any amount of visual information. The illustration styles and the images themselves can be thoughtfully chosen to convey exactly the right mood or feeling.

"...given talent and graphic skills, good packaging can be created without modern technical aids and gimmicks."

I think what continues to fascinate me is how it is possible for a particular visual quality of image to go on promoting a product to generation after generation, without its becoming dated. There is a museum at Grasse in the South of France which displays packaging, some of it more than 200 years old. I found it quite inspirational. The beauty and charm inherent in the use of illustration and typography have not been diminished by the primitive print processes of some

of the early work. It demonstrated to me that these early artists and designers were quite capable of creating an image that reflected quality and integrity, and it was also a rare opportunity to see how print has evolved over several centuries and how these new techniques were incorporated into the design work of the time.

What seems to me most important about this work, however, is that if these products were available today, their visual presentation would no doubt ensure their great success, which leads me to believe that, given talent and graphic skills, good packaging can be created without modern technical aids and gimmicks. I'm sure I am not the only one who is aware, because of this historical legacy, of how design appears to go in cycles. I have seen packaging for major companies go through bold contemporary themes and back to more delicate traditional ideas. Today the current trend, in my view, is for an individual, "exclusive" feel.

There is no point, however, in creating a design that is out

of context for its market, whatever the prevailing fashion – the design of the pack alone will not make a successful product. The product must also be of the same high quality, and it has to be marketed properly – *where* the product is to be sold is vitally important, too.

Branding

There is a great deal of social consciousness surrounding packaging. Because of the powerful marketing of brand leaders, one of the most difficult jobs must be creating an own-brand vodka or gin for example. People may be prepared to drink the lesser known brand themselves but are often embarrassed or unwilling to offer it to guests. Are they afraid that they could be criticized for offering an inferior product to visitors? Ultimately, the own-brand product still has the edge on good value, lower price, and the reassurance of the known qualities of the store that stands behind it.

An own-brand product or the redesign of a single product from a range should not be designed as an individual item. It has to sit on the shelf

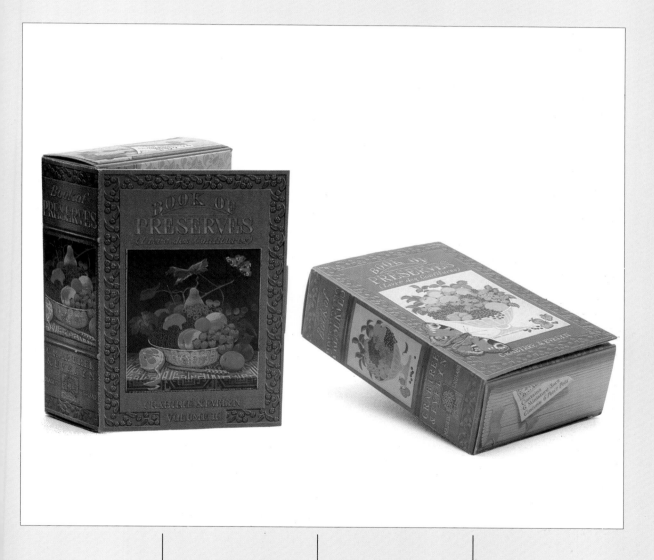

■ **Above** These charming packages for Crabtree and Evelyn preserves show how design and illustration can both enhance the image of the product and promote a company identity.

as a member of a family of products, so it must retain something of the identity of the existing group.

"If you can design images for posters or brochures, there is no reason why you should not be able to design a package."

As you become more familiar with packaging you will notice that products are often updated and repackaged. With own-brand package design there is a growing need to promote the quality appeal of these products. The redesign of packaging constitutes a major area of graphic design work. The client will not only be looking for increased sales – he will also hope to retain the customer loyalty he has built up with the old design. Creating a redesign will often be a pilot to monitor the sales of a product in advance of an overall change of image. There is usually only one opportunity to make a success of this – the repackaging of a single item is costly and astronomical when considered on a larger scale.

New products are usually approached differently, though. A great deal of careful research is done in advance to determine the public's perception before the final product finds its way onto the shelves. I recently designed the packaging for a new whisky – a particularly tricky project, as whisky drinkers have a strong brand loyalty, and the images used for packaging these products are firmly set in the consciousness of the customer. I presented five separate ideas, two of which I felt were very strong. These were then tested by the research companies before any final packaging was created.

"I look for intelligence, consistency, excellent presentation, and all forms of good draftsmanship."

Naturally, advertising assists in the communication of your product. The whisky market, for instance, is highly competitive, and while you must be looking to appeal to the next generation, you must not run the risk of alienating your established customers. It is important, therefore, that

the advertising campaign and the imagery it uses be complementary to the package design and the product itself.

Work in packaging design

Students entering the graphic design business, unless hell-bent on doing packaging, should stay general in their work to allow greater options. If you can design images for posters or brochures, there is no reason why you should not be able to design a package. Do not worry about the engineering of your bottle or container, as you will be able to seek advice should the image you have created be accepted. The graphic design industry needs new ideas all the time, so students should be looking forward and have open minds. Seek out new ideas – do not just imitate what is around.

I think it is important that ideas themselves usually do not change; it is the way they are expressed that makes them different. I remember passing the Christmas window of a large store and was stopped by the way the

Christmas theme had been interpreted by art college students – there was not a Santa Claus or reindeer to be seen. Instead there were examples of festivities from the four corners of the earth. There was no mistaking that it represented Christmas but the interpretation stood out, as it did not rely on traditional clichés.

Students' folios should reflect their personality and an individual approach to their work. There is no one ingredient that will make a successful portfolio. I look for intelligence, consistency, excellent presentation, and all forms of good draftsmanship. One student who came to show me her work found it necessary to *sing* the words that were an integral part of her visual presentations. Although this was a slightly bizarre approach, I was so impressed with her work and her performance that I recommended her to a close associate who hired her immediately.

Packaging: INTRODUCTION

The selling of packaged goods today relies on the strength of their visual presence. Although this is true of all packaging – from expensive perfume to car accessories – it is especially so in the luxury drinks market, where traditional brands have established their own visual associations with patterns of social behavior. A project of this kind relies on the graphic designer's ability to tap into an audience that has surplus income, enjoys socializing, and keeps up with fashions and trends. Influences such as the accessibility of overseas travel and the pleasant associations of people enjoying their free time, also have a role to play in the shaping of the concept.

The other major factor in pack design is image. The important difference between this and most other forms of graphic design is that this work offers an opportunity to think in a three-dimensional context. Unlike a design that relies on surface format and composition within that format, the product can be seen as a naked object that is to be "dressed" in a way that fits its image.

Because the design will be seen from many angles, it is necessary to assess how the surface graphics will work. Technical considerations will also influence the final ideas, although these constraints should be considered only after a solution has been found, for the design and the product's appearance are usually more important.

Branding

Research will be required into visual branding. The purpose of this will be to identify the visual associations of your own and similar, competitive products. You need to look at different age groups and social classes, why one product is more popular than another, and try to analyze what makes it so.

The choice of name – one already established, or a newly branded product – will influence the way you proceed in creating a design, for it will convey, by its sound and perhaps by its connotations, a sense of the product's inherent qualities. Your graphics will also be used in every aspect of the promotional material associated with the product: in magazines, television, and also point-of-sale promotion. The shape of the pack will also define the image, and by selecting the right shape, it is possible to send a particular message to your audience.

Basic lessons

The first aspect of this project asks the student to consider the name. This is unusual: the name would normally be supplied to the designer, who would work the design around it. This exercise will reveal the complexities of finding the name that sounds exactly right for the product. Don't ignore the fact that the name often needs to work across international boundaries.

The next area to be tested is the student's ability to think and visualize in three-dimensions. Here it is important to remember that the look of graphics changes when they are applied to surfaces or around a shape.

From this project the student should also gain a knowledge of how to create a continuity through the arrangement of individual elements on separate parts of the packaging. Where the package – a bottle, for example – requires an outer container, this will need to retain the qualities of the overall concept.

■ **Timeless design** This tin, designed c. 1890 for Lazzaroni, works as well today as it did when it was first produced.

T I P S

■ Choose your audience first. Look at their current drinking habits and at the images they relate to.
■ Research the recent successes in the market.
■ Invent the product name before attempting any designs.
■ Allow the name to control the visual concept.
■ Use an existing bottle for your mock-up. There's nothing to say you can't change the color of the bottle.
■ If adding color to the product, choose one that looks appealing and fruity.

Packaging: PRODUCT RESEARCH

Never are the stakes so high as when working on a project of this kind. Unlike other graphic areas – the production of a letterhead or brochure, for example – the design of this kind of packaging has a direct influence on the sales of the product itself. If the graphics are inappropriate they cannot just be discarded or even simply redesigned as they are the embodiment of the product.

It is for this reason that the design research must be followed thoroughly, and the designer should have accurate insight into the marketability of his or her own ideas. This job asks for a specific market to be targeted, and in this differs from previous projects in which students have been given a wider net, so there is all the more pressure to find the right styling for the particular market sector.

The 18–24 male/female group's income and social and cultural habits differ enormously from those of the group who are over 36 years of age, so consider the market you intend to target compared to the others specified. Pinpoint the differences between these groups, and make notes on their various areas of activity so that you can cross-refer easily. What is "corny" and unfashionable to one group may be attractive and familiar to another. Beware of the trap of categorizing each of the groups too rigidly, as there may be overlapping aspirations and similarities in taste that can be capitalized on. You will probably discover a mass of potential buyers who are typical of your target, with pockets of potential buyers who are not. The only way to confirm this is to carry out interviews and research in the field.

Once you know the background to the various market groups and trends you can focus your attention on a specific market and begin to consider likely names or word associations that could provide a name for your product. The name itself is unlikely to

PACKDESIGN ASSIGNMENT

The new product is 24 per cent proof and made from a blend of fruit essences and spices. The drink is devoid of color, but will be marketed in a suitable color.

The first stage of this project is to research the drinks market, paying particular attention to why new brands have been successful. Choose an audience category for your product from the following:
a   18–24 years, male or female.
b   24–36 years, female.
c   36 + years, male or female.
Back-up research may be necessary to confirm your choice of audience.

Design requirements
Using existing stock bottles, design a package that includes a product name and image, a product description, and labeling and packaging graphics to give the product a distinctive and unique identity.

Technical requirements
Take into consideration the product-display aspect of your design, as it will be appearing with other products on the shelf. Make sure the name is visible. Certain color additives to the drink are inadvisable. Natural fruit colors will enhance the appearance, whereas colors not normally associated with fruit, such as brown or blue, may appear unappetizing and even unhealthy.

For presentation purposes a full-size pack will be required, so make sure that it is sealed properly to prevent the destruction of your graphics.

■ **Student B**
Finding a name Visual associations with words were explored from which the shape of the bottle was developed. The student was looking for a name that worked both visually and aurally.

■ **Student A**
Finding a name This student started by developing ideas for a name. The product image was later shaped around the chosen name so this preliminary research proved to be instrumental in ensuring the right market image.

Secret
Romantic
Dangerous
Civilized

S
B
M
M
E
ME

Le CO

MAH
POTIO
A

demagnac

DEMAGNAC

appintaf

D'A

L'Ap

Grenoble
Geneva
France
Austria
Asia
Spain
Romania
Russia

ISSA SOSVA
   KIMRY
  TESHA
  TUGUR

   SURA
   RAMON

■ **Visual ideas** A number of alternative names, each suggesting a different image, were tried in the search for the most suitable option.

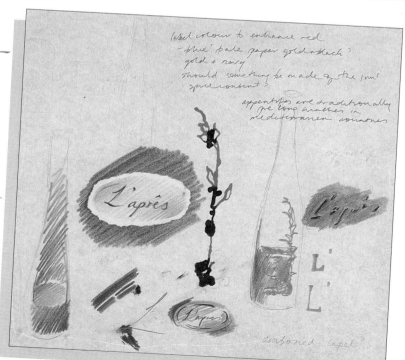

MAGNA

deme tasse
demian fer
apperit
apperau
appellus
appeline
appellout
apperause
   appeaux
   apperamon

L'aprés

■ **First ideas** The first sketches explored a theme of red and gold. A soft pinkish-red was used together with gold, producing an image suggestive of luxury and quality. The French name immediately influenced the product's profile.

Continued on next page

be found by studying dictionaries, as it is more likely to be a word that associates itself either with the visual concept or with the idea of pleasurable experiences (and in so doing stimulates a feeling of comfort or well-being). In short, it should be a name that is easy to remember, suggests enjoyment.

Bear in mind other factors influencing your product, such as, in the 1990s, the concern with healthy eating and natural foods and the recent decline in consumption of strong alcoholic drinks in favor of wine and non-alcoholic alternatives.

Think of words or places that you would associate with your market, and below these key words list alternative ideas. Look at the potential of each of these ideas and see if they trigger off other flights of the imagination into areas as yet unexplored. Try out these words on the selected audience, and assess their reactions.

Words and image

Once likely product names have emerged, you can start thinking visually. This stage will also involve the selection of the container for your drink. In your research you will have discovered the shapes and proportions of containers that are available; it is now a question of linking these to some visual idea. Do the potential product names give you any clues?

Thumbnail sketches can now be made, and ideas can be applied to the shapes. Note that the stress is on ideas and not labels. The concept should look part of the package and not be merely a stick-on shape. The styling should affect the bottle from top to bottom.

Remember that many techniques or materials can be applied to the surface of the container at this stage of the project and later refined by graphic control. Envision the design around the bottle by making in-

dividual drawings from different angles. Explore how the graphics will work on the back and the front – all aspects of your design should work together.

You will probably find, once you have made some initial sketches, that you need to take stock of what is emerging. Your chosen name may need further research to amend or adjust the sound, or the visual approach may need further thought and research. Some consonants in your first choice of name may be too harsh for your chosen image, or, inappropriately, too soft. Maybe the name you have chosen has a modern ring but retrospective connotations. Perhaps there is a national identity to the emerging product which needs to be encouraged to tease out its full potential.

It may not be easy to find relevant typefaces, and in order to establish the right visual idea it may even be necessary to design a typeface specifically for this product.

Once the concept is formed and the word is right, the choice of color and styling can begin. You will find that different locations and various sizes for the name can be tried, with the result that even the subtlest change can influence the overall effect. A hint of blue will shift a color from the warm range into the cool. Even the reflection from the back of a label may affect the color in the bottle.

The printing need not be on the label; it could be applied directly to the surface of the bottle. It could even be etched or raised from the surface of the glass itself. Indeed, ask yourself whether the container needs to be made of glass at all. Are there other materials that would fit the desired image while giving the product a unique edge in the market?

Consider also how you can educate your audience into trying new ideas and new

■ **Student A**
3 container shapes In order to develop an identity, the student first generated some ideas about the shape of the container. Clearly, a decision about the intended target group was also important, since this would have a bearing on the shape.

■ **Student B**
Image building The student continued to develop ideas about both the label and the name. The name "D'avance" was chosen, partly for its visual potential. It offered the opportunity to develop an elegant "D," touching on the associations this prefix has with the names of noble French families. The overall image was evolving as a drink for a discerning market.

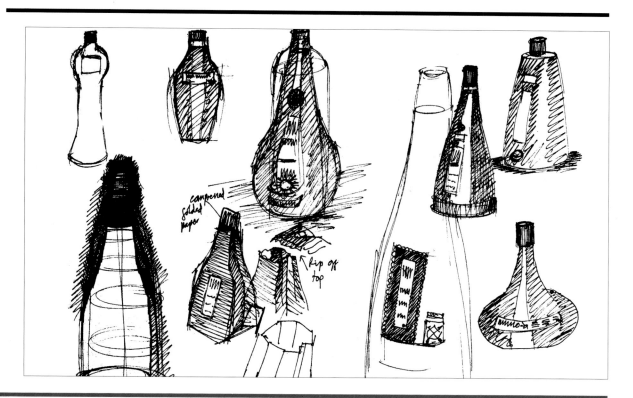

L'apeit

D'avence   D'Avance   The perfect beginning   D'AVANCE

products. Sometimes a novelty value can motivate a new audience to make a purchase. However, a danger to be guarded against when taking this route is that the product itself may be cheapened. Also, as a fashion object, its popularity will be very short-lived.

Once an idea is established, check how it works in full size on the container itself. There is no better test in this kind of work than studying the actual product, since drawings can only give an impression of the design. The refinements need to happen on the model itself, and it may even be necessary to place it among competitive products to see how the image compares. Again, your own market research is useful here, for by testing the name and the product's visual impact you can quickly make an appraisal of the design's effectiveness.

Product accessories

On examining your product, which should now have the right name and the right image for that name, you may discover that some small detail is lacking. It could be on the container itself, such as a special cap, or maybe something to adorn the bottle itself, such as a seal or medal. Or the container and its design may work perfectly but require the addition of an outer case or container.

This refinement opens up various possibilities: the outer case can become a carrying case for a single purchase or many purchases, or an elegant, stylish package reminiscent of a special gift. If it is elegance or sophistication you are seeking, a special feeling can be lent by the choice of material itself — for example, it may suggest silk, leather, or even solid rock. There are many

■ **Student A**
Toward the final image
"Sura" was chosen as the product name, offering a dark, mysterious image. The container needed to reflect this sense of mystery, and the student devised an outer pack that would help provide this. The graphics on the bottle were to be minimal, but the drink has been colored to give a dark, rich quality with a hint of freshness.

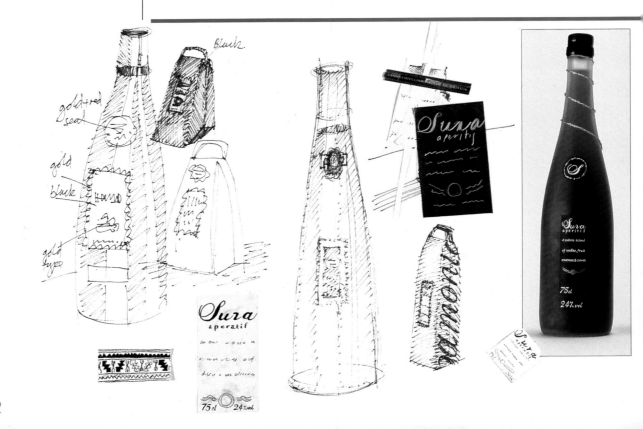

modern papers from which the designer can choose, from simulated leather to marbled surfaces. It could be that the season plays an important part in the sales of this product, and if so, you will need to consider the image accordingly.

As the product develops, the image can be applied to other display items, such as point-of-sale show cards and posters. Although the brief does not require this, all kinds of marketing support will have to be developed. Make sure your design is versatile enough to work for other aspects of display.

Photographing a presentation

This may appear to be a simple task, but planning pack-shot photography is essential. Getting the lighting right and achieving the most dynamic visual effect may call for some skillful photographic techniques. For instance, when photographing glass the position of the lighting is crucial, as wrongly directed light will create flare, which will destroy your design.

The photographic image is likely to be the presentation you make to the client; it needs to be carefully considered so that it shows the design in the right atmosphere. A hasty snapshot is useless even as reference material.

Usually graphic designers are not expected to handle a camera and the complex equipment professionally, since a photographer would normally be commissioned to photograph the work at such an important stage. But remember, you are still in control of the images you wish the photographer to create, and it is *your* design that must convince the client.

The final idea The finished design was now formulated as a rough visual which would guide the final refinement of detail and set a pattern for the creation of the presentation pack.

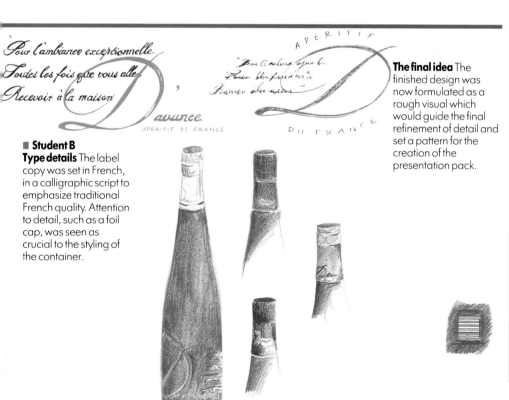

■ **Student B**
Type details The label copy was set in French, in a calligraphic script to emphasize traditional French quality. Attention to detail, such as a foil cap, was seen as crucial to the styling of the container.

Critique

The three presentations shown here each have qualities that make them both attractive and stylish. The client was looking for a formula that would reflect people's changing drinking habits, as evidenced by the changes taking place in the market. The specific groups targeted were: 18–24 year-old male and female; 24–36 year-old female; and 36 + years, male and female.

Because the projects were produced by students who fall into the first category, the project represented a considerable challenge to them to understand an audience with much wider personal experience than themselves. How well the students aimed the product at their chosen target group is best assessed by analyzing the research carried out by each.

Although the individual designs are supported by a specific written profile, common factors were uncovered in the preparation of this background work. The students felt that a new healthier attitude toward alcohol was emerging from all the age groups. With an increasing interest being shown in quality food and wine at dinner parties and a new awareness of the dangers of drinking and driving, the consumption of traditional strong alcoholic drinks such as whisky and gin is in decline. The research indicated a need for lighter, less alcoholic beverages which promote sociability and complement new eating habits. The drink was discovered to offer a fruity, pleasant flavor, and left no aftertaste. This seemed to make it an ideal candidate as a pre-dinner aperitif.

All the students felt that the drink should have a branding style with a European or otherwise foreign appearance. The idea of French quality featured prominently in two of the designs, as the students felt that such an image displayed a seriousness about the quality of the product. This concept also links to the increasing adoption of French drinking habits – in particular the taking of a light aperitif as a preliminary to the meal. This way of using alcohol suggests sophistication, and the styling of the product in two of the presentations was intended to exploit this quality.

Although the two designs give the product a distinctive, elegant identity with their slim traditional wine-bottle shape, there is a feeling that by using this container the product has immediate associations with wine and not stronger alcohol. This international use of an established product image, such as quality wine, may conflict with the reality of the product itself. Bear in mind that a bottle of wine is normally consumed at one sitting, unlike the aperitif, which is usually served in small glasses and then returned to the drinks cabinet for another occasion.

The product names

The names chosen for this product, Sura, Chimera and D'avance, deserve attention, as they have to a large extent determined the look of these presentations.

Sura has a mystique that echoes the Far East. It was hit upon by thinking of an image that conjured up words such as "secret," "romantic," "dangerous," and "civilized." The use of black and gold strung around the body of the design is sensual. The student decided that the product needed an outer container, and the mystery and sense of secrecy are captured in a simple stylish carrying box, on the surface of which the name of the product is hinted at with embossed letters.

This student chose a deep but refreshing red for the product which appears chilled in the frosted bottle. The simplicity of the overall design, although attractive, does not give the product the authority it requires to

■ **Student A**
Sura The gold braid veiling the frosted glass surface has a sensuous quality. The name and the contents are subtly displayed on a small label, with the volume and alcoholic content prominently displayed. The box container is almost too subtle, and the product needs more identification.

succeed commercially.

The next product, D'avance, relies heavily on its French name. This image is carried through with simplicity and sophistication, and the product has a regal and refreshing visual appeal. The color used for the drink, a peachy rose, suggests a light, drinkable refreshment. The graphics and the calligraphic letterforms are applied directly to the surface of the frosted-glass bottle. The "D" becomes an excellent device, giving an identity to the overall product. The name D'avance offers considerable scope for the promotional material that would support a product of this kind.

The use of gold, white, and red for the bottle conveys the luxury and quality you would expect from a quality product, but the overall image needs to be viewed against the competition. It is one of many on the market and needs something to set it apart.

Finally, Chimera is obviously aimed at a younger audience. Its trendy graphics are designed to suggest decorative, young fashions. A sense of quality is conveyed by this image, which appeals mainly to a young, aware audience. The image does not try to disguise the fact that the drink contains alcohol. The bottle is reminiscent of those used for stronger drinks and has a solid presence. The liquid itself is presented in its original clear form and invites experimentation with other ingredients. Its jazzy appearance departs from the traditional way of packaging alcoholic drinks and has a distinctly fun appeal. The name has an attractive ring to it, and the various ways in which it might be pronounced could give rise to a gentle game of one-upmanship among its drinkers. The image gives the product two distinct but complementary angles. The bottle shape indicates hard liquor, while the graphics appear light and refreshing.

■ **Student B**
D'avance The gold and white applied directly on the frosted glass surface is set off beautifully by the deep rose pink color of the drink. The bottle cap adds to this with the metallic rose pink foil sealed with a gold strip. The balance of the graphics looks professional and confident, although visually the packaging looks more like a quality rosé wine than an apéritif.

■ **Student C**
Chimera This entirely different approach suggests a strong liquor like vodka or schnapps. On closer inspection the label design uses a Cubist or Constructivist illustration. The cool use of color in association with the white frosted glass bottle looks strong, young in image, and masculine. For the design to succeed, it would need to be carefully refined.

Advertising: SEMINAR

BILLY MAWHINNEY, the Joint Creative Director of J. Walter Thompson, London.

My career began in Belfast working for Ordnance Survey, then the Public Housing Authority, and as a paste-up man for a design group. But because I had no training, I became aware that my career was going nowhere. So having worked in the real world, I decided to go to art college in Belfast and learn all the graphic skills I think you need to be successful in the graphic design business.

"to be successful in graphics and advertising you must have strong craft skills."

Three years later, as a qualified graphic designer, I was taken on by J Walter Thompson in London as a trainee art director. After two years, finding London unsettling, I returned to Belfast to teach in the same college. I enjoyed this period; despite my short career, it gave me some practical experience to offer. One of the most important lessons I was taught was that to be successful in graphics and advertising you must have strong craft skills. I have since learned, as an employer of art directors, that the best in the industry have good graphic skills in addition to their lively, creative minds. They are capable of seeing an idea through from concept to visual. John Hegarty, of Bartle Bogle Hegarty, is a prime example: he would expect his art directors to recognize the subtleties of type and image and to know why a

■ **Above** An early conceptual rough for a campaign advertising Polo mints.

hold onto.

The mint with the hold.

ble. When the art director needs to employ a chain of experts, he becomes a liability.

Good teamwork

In an advertising agency today, you will probably find teams who work together. The team consists of an art person and a copy person, so you find art directors normally come in pairs, one concentrating on words and the other on images. Some agencies

"advertising is not about formulae, it is about good ideas."

have creative teams on the go almost around the clock to produce a stream of work which is then selected or rejected by the creative director. While it is the creative director's job to decide if the work is good enough, this "sausage machine" method tends to deprive the individual of the responsibility they should take for their work. It also makes it more difficult for a young designer to learn from the process, thereby improving his or her work.

particular image worked and how to improve it. Often there is no time to ask the opinion of others; the art director must know how to make the visuals

as well as the concept work. He can only do this job properly if he knows his trade. I think over recent years some art directors have become

too reliant on the support of, say, a typographer, or an illustrator, or a photographer. In the current economic climate this is no longer possi-

It is more difficult for young teams these days to be trained within the agency itself. When I started as a trainee art director, I was able to observe the senior staff at work. Nowadays, agencies are more likely to hire fully fledged art directors. This makes it difficult for students aspiring to a job in advertising. Art colleges tend to teach students design by formulas and advertising is not about formulas, it is about good ideas. Nor is it about producing slick advertisements that copy existing images. Students make the rounds with portfolios showing strong visuals with a selling strapline which are well executed, but they all look the same. What advertising needs is original thinking, and this does not come out of providing ads you think the creative director wants to see, but from you finding something you want to say.

"you do not have to be...a martyr...just...do your job well and work hard."

Whatever your brief, your job is to communicate, to interest people, and not talk

As you hang onto that strap, swaying through the tunnel, you might well be forgiven for wondering how a Polo Mint could ever help you keep your balance. Well, we would have to admit that it would take a lot more than a full tube of Polos to keep anyone upright in a full tube train at full speed. But, if you've got yourself a seat, then you might just find it useful to have something to hold onto, instead of

SOMETHING TO HOLD ONTO

twiddling your thumbs. And what could be better than a tube of Polo Mints. Just pop one off the top and pop it in your mouth. Hold the tube to keep your hands in place and the cool refreshing mint can have a beneficial effect on your mental equilibrium too. Thus secured, both mentally and physically, throw caution to the wind and offer one to the person sitting next to you. Polo, the mint with the hold.

down to them. You should know precisely what response to your product you want to elicit, and the advertising you create should stimulate this response. Remember, your audience will not be interested in your product unless and until you can hold their attention for long enough to *make* them interested. To do this, your work must be fresh and original. This cannot be achieved with formulas. You need to get into an agency to discover this for yourself. Even a student can call a top agency and ask whether you can make the coffee for a week and get a feel for what is really going on.

When I lecture at art colleges, I find it surprising how much interest there is; and how enthusiastic the students appear to be. Yet I hear from

very few students afterwards. If you get yourself a contact, like myself, and you are not knocking on the door the next day, I don't believe you are truly interested in advertising. I have known students to rent the windows opposite top creative directors' offices to display their ads in the hope that they will be seen. There is no doubt about the commitment of *these* young hopefuls!

As in any job, to be successful you have to set out to be good. A professional footballer, who wants to play well on a Saturday, must train hard during the week. Advertising has to be approached in the same way: to produce good ads you must be professional and efficient. You cannot expect to stroll in at 10:30 a.m. and then take two hours for lunch. I have always

used John Hegarty as an example of professionalism in the business. He manages to create some of the best advertisements in a normal working day. In other words, you do not have to be a hero and a martyr to the advertisement cause. You just have to do your job well and work hard.

I have heard young people say that they think they will go into advertising for a few years with the intention of becoming a film producer. I find it difficult to conceal a smile. This is definitely the wrong attitude. If you want to make films, go to film school. But if someone walked into my office who was good and enthusiastic, I would clear a space to give them a job.

■ **Above** The final poster in the Polo campaign.

Advertising: INTRODUCTION

In addition to his or her visual skills, the graphic designer needs an extra ingredient to succeed in advertising. He or she must develop the ability to sell a product or service through visuals and words to a selected group of people.

The role of the advertising agency is principally to create press and TV advertising. This also includes magazine and trade advertising. Unlike graphic design consultancies, the agency's major income does not come directly from creative output. It is from "billing." This is the percentage paid to the agency by the client and is based on the fees paid for advertising in newspapers and magazines. So when a client buys an advertisement, he pays full price for the space and the agency takes a commission. A good, creative in-house team can pitch for and handle other areas of work, too. These include large poster campaigns, brochure and leaflet work, and often point-of-sale and display work.

The industry is split up into different categories of work, with multi-national manufacturers of consumer goods spending big money on well-produced TV and national press advertising. Endowed with advertising budgets running into millions, this work is perceived as the most glamorous. Such companies are known as blue-chip clients.

To graduate to the role of art director on blue-chip accounts, the young designer would most probably start his career working on smaller accounts (i.e. smaller in terms of billing), or as a junior member of a large creative team. Because the work can cover a variety of graphic commissions, a versatile, well-trained graphic designer wanting to break into advertising will benefit here. He would be involved in the preparation of small, local, and national advertisements as well as leaflets, posters, brochures, point-of-sale displays, and all other material which is required in the sales and promotion of the product or service.

Who's who in the team

The advertising industry is divided into a number of functions. A typical agency employs several account executives, whose role is to find clients for the agency and then service these accounts. They work with the creative teams, consisting of an art director and a copywriter. Their function is to create concepts with visuals and words. There is no actual demarcation of responsibilities, and, clearly, there are times when these two roles merge. The best teams operate in tandem, by each complementing the other's ability – the copywriter's skill with words and the art director's visual sense.

These creative teams are supported by experts in various disciplines: to back up the art director, the agency employs visualizers to create client presentations. There may also be some specialist typographers on hand to assist in the layout of type. The art director is, of course, perfectly capable of carrying out these tasks himself; the support team is there to leave him free to concentrate on creative concepts for the individual campaigns.

The agency will also employ production teams whose job it is to ensure that all the agency's print and advertising needs are artworked and produced within budget, on time, and to the high standard of the client.

The agency's key man or woman is the creative director, who is in overall control of the creative output. It is his or her job to hire and fire all of the creative staff, monitor the work being produced, offer overall creative guidance, and maintain the agency's reputation in the marketplace.

T I P S

- Good, strong selling ideas are what you need for your advertisements to succeed.
- Your message has to be conveyed instantly.
- Visual impact is important but concepts come first.
- Advertising needs new ideas and new approaches.

Advertising: CAMPAIGNS

Every day thousands of advertisements appear in newspapers and magazines, each with the purpose of selling a service or product. With all these individual images fighting to attract your attention, you can appreciate how vital it is to create advertisements that are noticed, understood, and stand out from the mass.

When someone buys a newspaper or magazine, their primary interest is in the news stories, the editorials, and the sports pages. To be successful, your advertisement must stop the reader in their tracks and redirect their attention to the information you want them to read. You have only a split second in which to do this. There will be no salesman present to persuade the reader to buy the product or service you are promoting: your advertisement must work alone.

What makes a product or service different from – and therefore more desirable than – another is a USP, a Unique Selling Proposition. It does not matter if this difference is small, just so long as it is different. You are looking for something to turn into an advantage. It is possible that your client's product or service is cheaper, or bigger, or smaller than the competition. It is for you to find this USP.

Promoting the product

You must then be selective about what you wish to say about your product. Mention only the facts that support your case. Think of a lawyer in court: the defense will create a case to prove the defendant innocent, while the prosecution will attempt to establish guilt. Both lawyers will select only the facts that support their point of view. Similarly you will have to pinpoint the features that promote your product or service in the best light. For instance, if your client's product is cheaper than a competitor, the advertisement might

ADVERTISING
ASSIGNMENT

Choose one of the following assignments:

A. Promotion of safe foods. The client is Parents for Safe Food.

Campaign and design requirements
Point out to parents, manufacturers, and retailers that there is now a watchdog that will expose the use and misuse of chemicals in foods. Create whole page, black and white advertisements (including 48 sheet posters, TV and bus sides).

B. Promotion for specialist clothes retailer. The client is High and Mighty, which specializes in quality outsize male fashions.

Campaign and design requirements
The full-color poster campaign should communicate to outsize males that there is a specialist retailer just for them.

■ **Student team A**
Concept sheets The team investigated where pesticides and poisonous sprays are used. They decided to use a strong visual message with a simple, direct copyline. The approach to visuals needs to be simple at this stage, to test the ideas. The standard of visual (right) is still quite high for the beginnings of a campaign.

We can clothe a man up to a 60 inch chest

HIGH & MIGHTY
Quality clothes for large men

When pesticides are sprayed on to fruit it doesn't just stay on the surface

Parents for safe food .

We sell the widest range of large clothes

HIGH & MIGHTY

HIGH & MIGHTY
Quality clothes for large men

■ **Student team B Concept sheets** The initial concepts on the outsize clothing assignment went straight to the point using copy that immediately commun-icated the nature of the business, and images that pulled no punches. The USP of this retailer — that they sell big clothes — is immediately obvious from these visuals.

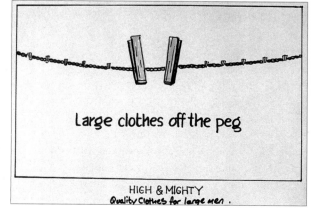

Large clothes off the peg

HIGH & MIGHTY
Quality clothes for large men .

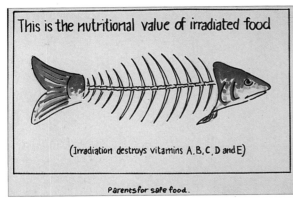

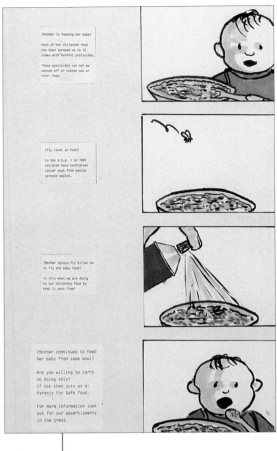

■ Student team A
Choosing a medium
The fish idea was developed as a large format poster. The mother offering a spoon, for use in press advertisements, invites the viewer to get involved.

■ Introducing type
The fish poster was further developed using tasteful typography and illustration to introduce a distasteful subject.

■ Storyboard for TV
For TV a storyboard for a commercial was developed. A sequence of events was devised that pinpointed one aspect of the pesticide problem. The team has only shown four of the images for this sequence. It parodies what actually happens to food before it reaches the table. The mother spraying pesticide into the child's bowl alarms the viewer especially when the child continues to eat. A set of TV storyboards need only describe the essence of the message. Detail comes later in the script.

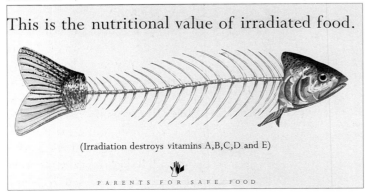

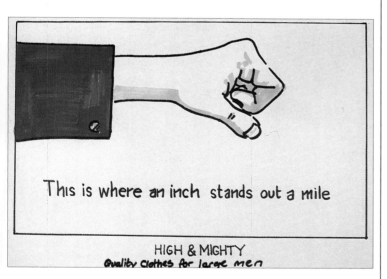

■ Student team B
Further concepts The team explored further ideas, here devising an approach to tell the reader that he no longer has to accept ill-fitting clothes whatever size he is. The visuals state this message clearly, while the headlines provoke thought. The campaign strapline for all the posters has been kept consistent. The loose drawings have been produced in marker and are more than sufficient to describe the ideas.

read: "Why pay more?" If your product is more expensive it could say: "Buy the Best." In the same way, if you are selling a glass of water that is half empty, you could say, quite truthfully, that it is half full, and a product that is common could also be called "popular"! It is important not to be dishonest in the claims you make about your product – this is illegal. The most successful campaigns are those you can believe in because they make sense. Do not try to be too clever. As you gain experience you can experiment. As you can see, your campaign strategy has little to do with graphic design at this stage, it is all about creative ideas and concepts.

The client's brief will set out the parameters within which you have to work. If the budget is small, it will be necessary to consider carefully the media in which your advertisement is to appear. To assist in this task the agency employs media planners, who buy space. With their expertise you can establish the right location and the most suitable medium for your client's advertisement. For example, a poster campaign, appearing on the sides of buses, billboards and on displays within public transportation, might best suit the concept and the budget allocated to the job. The right choice in the right position ensures that you will hit the selected target.

Visual presentation

Once the concept has been formulated, the next step is to create the campaign itself. This aspect of the work requires a large graphic input, for it is now that a series of themes are produced by designers to support the basic sales message. The ideas for this will need to exploit the concept, delivering the message each time in an effective and resourceful manner. You will be looking for ways to hold your audience's attention, and hopefully encourage them to identify with the other advertisements in the campaign. You know your campaign is successful when people start talking about it.

As with other graphic design areas your approach must be bold, professional, and disciplined. The initial ideas need only be thumbnail sketches, followed by more careful visual developments.

Succeeding in advertising

The character of the advertising industry continues to change to meet modern requirements. The 1980s saw a boom in direct advertising: selling off the page and by mailing campaigns. Specialist agencies have been set up which still rely on creative skills but place an increasing importance upon graphic presentation.

Creativity and good ideas are the major input into advertising work. Graphic design skills are essential to support these ideas and to present them most effectively. Specialist areas of work, such as direct mail, require a high level of graphic design skill, although the concepts stand or fall by their degree of innovation or originality.

There are no short cuts to learning how to create effective advertising campaigns. Study the subject and analyze the advertisements in print and on television. Look at the content of the ads. Do they work, and could you think of a better idea for promoting the product? Talk to those who know how to create successful advertising.

The selection of work in your portfolio or "book" should demonstrate that you understand, and have some experience of, the advertising business. If you wish eventually to become an art director, your portfolio will need to include several advertising campaigns. These should be selected to reflect your skills in creating concepts, so it is

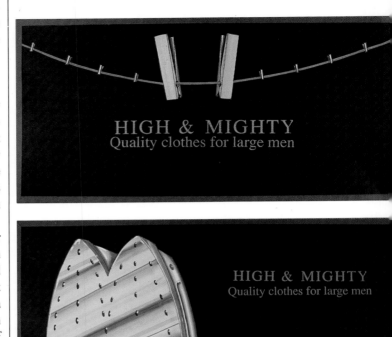

■ **Student team B** **The right idea for the medium** The final versions of the billboard posters have now been synthesized into a form that expects the viewer to interpret them. The written puns on the concept sheets have been dropped, and the company name and the sub-head have been moved into a prime position. The visual puns are left to convey their own message. The qualities depicted in these marker visuals add sophistication.

The fact is we feed our children far too many dangerous chemicals. Much of the food we feed them contains additives that have not been tested. As a result of this 1300 people die every year and many others will suffer from serious related illnesses. Alarming levels of pesticide residue have been found in foods we would normally consider healthy. At least 22% of these pesticides are suspected or known to cause cancer.

Where do most children get hold of dangerous chemicals

No caring parent would feed their children food which could poison them. But thanks to official secrecy we are all guilty of doing just that. At Parents For Safe Food we no longer want to be fed lies about our food.
The food industry, scientific advisors and even the government admit that some of the food we eat is unsafe. We will insist that industry, farmers and the government put health and safety before profit. If you would like to become a Parent For Safe Food yourself or just require more information on the subject we will be pleased to hear from you. Contact Parents For Safe Food, Britannia House, Hammersmith, London W6 0LF

P A R E N T S   F O R   S A F E   F O O D

How many times have you been told to wash fruit before you eat it. Unfortunately washing will only clean the surface. But an apple will soak up pesticide like a sponge, just as you will when you eat the apple. A typical English apple will be sprayed 12 times before you or your child eats it. If that wasn't reason enough not to buy one, consider that 22% of pesticides are known or suspected carcinogens (cancer inducing). In the U.S.A. 1 in every 1000 children have contracted cancer from eating pesticide ridden fruit. At Parents For Safe

When pesticides are sprayed on to fruit it doesn't just stay on the surface.

Food we want to make sure action is taken, before our children contract cancer. Like you, we are concerned about the safety of our childrens food, and we have good reason to be. The food industry, scientific advisors and even the government admit that some of the food we eat is unsafe. We will insist that they put health and safely before profit. If you would like to become a Parent For Safe Food yourself or just require more information on the subject we will be pleased to hear from you. Contact Parents For Safe Food, Britannia House, Hammersmith, London W6 0LF

P A R E N T S   F O R   S A F E   F O O D

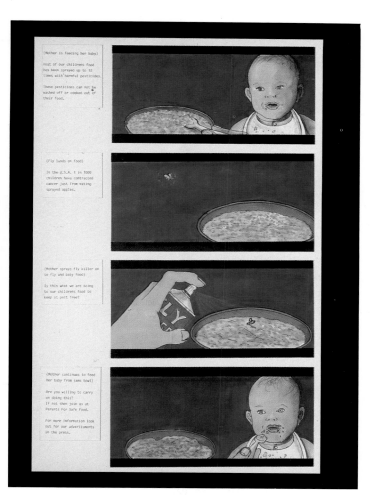

[Mother is feeding her baby]

Most of our childrens food has been sprayed up to 12 times with harmful pesticides.

These pesticides can not be washed off or cooked out of their food.

[Fly lands on food]

In the U.S.A. 1 in 1000 children have contracted cancer just from eating sprayed apples.

[Mother sprays fly killer on to fly and baby food]

Is this what we are doing to our childrens food to keep it pest free?

[Mother continues to feed her baby from same bowl]

Are you willing to carry on doing this? If not then join us at Parents For Safe food.

For more information look out for our advertisements in the press.

■ **Student team A**
Press advertisements In the final layout (left) the text has been written to fit the space. Headings occupy the same position for each of the advertisements. Note how the style is kept consistent through choice of layout, type, and illustration.

The TV storyboard has been refined visually and has been drawn in a form that can be presented to the client using markers.

Bus poster This is a good example of how the message can use the medium to make a point.

The driver of this bus had to pass a test.
The additives in your food didn't.

Parents for safe food

less important that they be highly finished in presentation form, as their purpose is to show that your work and your thinking are creative and original. Make sure that your portfolio displays the work in a logical fashion, for most agency creative directors will simply ask you to leave your portfolio, perhaps calling you back on another occasion.

If your interests were more in the direction of visualizing or typography in advertising, you will need a portfolio of extremely well presented and highly finished work. Agencies also require people in technical areas, such as illustrators, finishing artists, and paste-up specialists. Photographic retouchers are also in demand.

PROMOTIONAL ASSIGNMENT

The product is brown wrapping paper. The client is the British Post Office. This product has always been available but is rarely promoted or displayed, and its qualities have not been investigated. It is durable and is the right product for wrapping all kinds of parcels.

Design Requirements
A point of sale display which can be used as dispenser or hopper, so that paper can be sold in sheets or rolls.

Technical Requirements
Attractive three-dimensional display, inexpensive, lightweight, and space-saving.

■ **The concept** The student's concept for this product is "smart parcels would not want to be seen in anything else." The drawings on the worksheets (below and right) explore the feeling that personal objects can reflect brown paper's versatility and smartness. These drawings not only develop aesthetic ideas but also try to find practical solutions to storage and display.

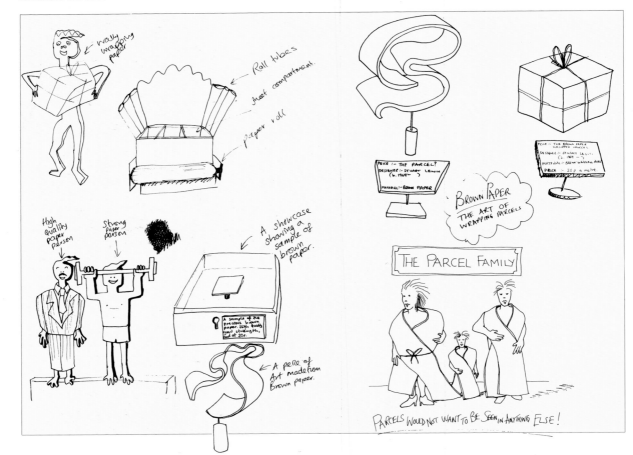

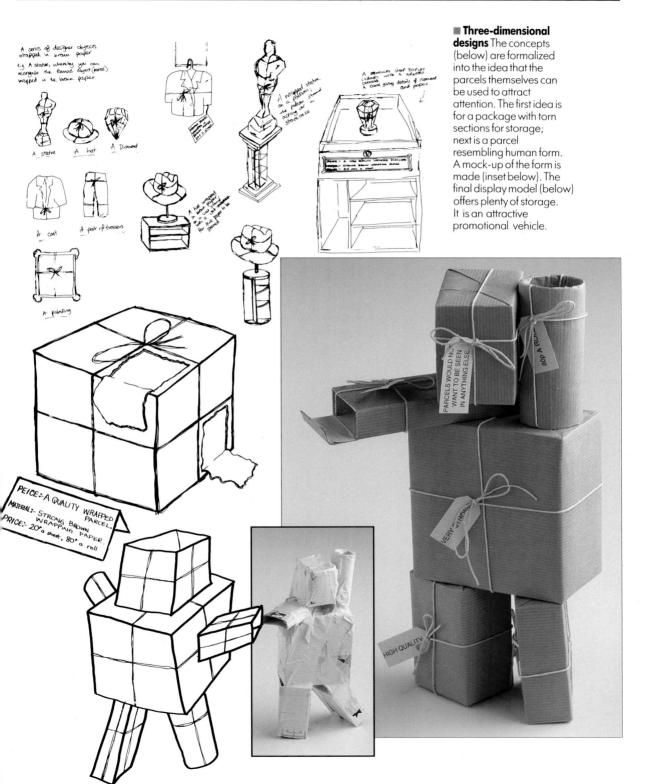

A series of designer objects wrapped in brown paper.

e.g. A statue, whereby you can recognise the famous object (parcel) wrapped in the brown paper.

A statue A hat A Diamond

A coat A pair of trousers

A painting

■ Three-dimensional designs The concepts (below) are formalized into the idea that the parcels themselves can be used to attract attention. The first idea is for a package with torn sections for storage; next is a parcel resembling human form. A mock-up of the form is made (inset below). The final display model (below) offers plenty of storage. It is an attractive promotional vehicle.

PEICE:- A QUALITY WRAPPED PARCEL.
MATERIAL:- STRONG BROWN WRAPPING PAPER.
PRICE:- 20° a sheet, 80° a roll

PARCELS WOULD NOT WANT TO BE SEEN IN ANYTHING ELSE.

VERY QUALITY

HIGH QUALITY

BOP A ROLL

177

DIRECT RESPONSE ASSIGNMENT

The client is a well established private school. For many years it has attracted serious students of garden design, history, and horticulture. The school recruits students on the strength of its reputation and through advertising in the gardening media.

Design Requirements
Create two mailing brochures. The first needs to be in the form of a leaflet or series of leaflets that announce short courses, visits, and lectures. The second is to be a full brochure describing the prestigious one-year course.

Technical Requirements
At present the school has no established design image except for its favored typeface. The assignment is open for interpretation, although limited color is advised.

The English Gardening School

Texture and quality This was developed (below) by manipulating more old prints of luxurious gardens with a photocopier.

■ **Student A**
New logo design The first student began by creating an image (above) that reflected the qualities of the school, using an old woodcut and a complementary typeface.

■ **Student B**
Existing logo design
This student has retained the old school type style and incorporated it into a design. A wrapping paper effect that repeats the image creates an interesting and eye-catching image.

■ **Portfolio** The student has created a portfolio, combining the logo and old prints, to add to the presentation of individual leaflets. The old print is photocopied onto the folio cover. Leaflets inside carry the same image, which has been lightened by diffusing it with tracing paper while photocopying.

Folder The repeated logo was used in the creation of a small folder (left), by photocopying it and cutting it out. This meant that leaflets could be easily revised and updated. The folder was designed to fit a standard business envelope and thus took into account the cost of mailing.

Leaflets Individual leaflets concerning each of the school's activities are inserted in the folder (left), enabling specialist mailings to be arranged.

Continued on next page

■ **Student A**
Brochure The next part of the student's work was to create a prestigious brochure for the one-year course. The brochure cover (right) follows the portfolio's theme by displaying the old print. The use of Bockingford watercolor paper adds quality and gives a textured surface. The portfolio's ribbons have been incorporated into the design to secure the pages.

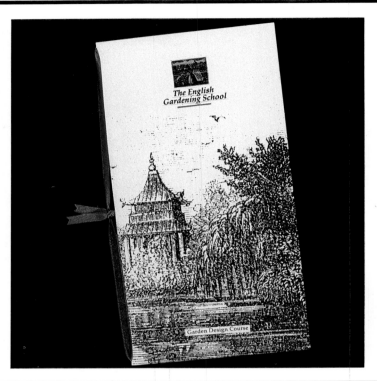

■ **Features** Elegant illuminated capitals draw attention to the text and are used as a device on the inner pages (below).

■ **Student B**
Brochure The logo device was carried through. The cover uses hand-made board. The inside pages use simple capital letters which echo the logo.

Summer season for bats

*G*ipsum dolor sit amet, consectetuer adipiscing elit diam zum nonnumy eiusmod tempor incidunt ut labore et dolore magna aliqua erat volupat. Ut enim ad minim veniam, quis nostrud exercitation nisi ut aliquip ex ea commodo consequat. Duis autem vel eum iriure dolor in reprehenderit in voluptate velit esse molestiae consequat, vel illum dolore eu fugiat nulla pariatur.

At vero eos et accusam et iusto odiom dignissim qui blandit praesent luptatum delenit aigue duos dolor et se molestias excepteur sint occaecat cupidat non provident, simil sunt it culpa qui officia deserunt mollit anim id est laborum et dolor fuga. Et harumd dereud facilis est er expedit distinct. Nam liber tempor cumet soluta nobis eligend optio.

Lrem ipsum dolor sit amet, consectetuer adipiscing elit, sed diam zum nonnumy eiusmod tempor incidunt ut labore et dolore magna aliqua erat volupat. Ut enim ad minim veniam, quis nostrud exercitation nisi ut aliquip ex ea commodo consequat. Duis autem vel eum iriure dolor in reprehenderit in voluptate velit esse molestiae consequat, vel illum dolore eu fugiat nulla pariatur.

At vero eos et accusam et iusto odiom dignissim qui blandit praesent luptatum delenit aigue duos dolor et se molestias excepteur sint occaecat cupidat non provident, simil sunt it culpa qui officia deserunt mollit anim id est laborum et dolor fuga. Et harumd dereud facilis est er expedit distinct. Nam liber tempor cumet soluta nobis eligend optio.

Inside The interior of the brochure is printed in green and black with heavy margins and reversed-out type at the top of the page. The overall theme is traditional elegance.

ASSIGNMENT

Create an insert that will be placed in a magazine. The client is a book club, and they wish to promote their books in a color leaflet offering a free book to any subscriber who introduces a friend or colleague. The insert must carry a first class prepaid reply coupon.

■ **Cover** The student has produced a very direct leaflet. It is a folded card with photographs and illustrations combined.

■ **Inside** The selling message is repeated, and includes information on how to apply for the free book.

■ **Back** The layout takes into account postal regulations for reply coupons.

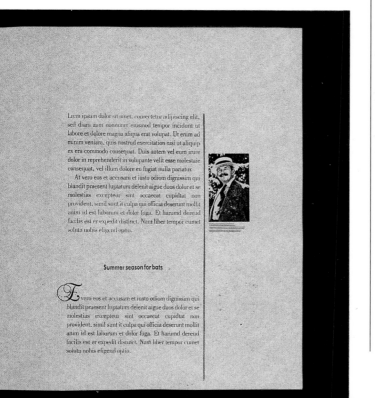

Lorem ipsum dolor sit amet, consectetur adipiscing elit, sed diam zum nonnumy eiusmod tempor incident ut labore et dolore magna aliqua erat volupat. Ut enim ad minim veniam, quis nostrud exercitation nisi ut aliquip ex era comnodo consequat. Duis autem vel eum irure dolor in reprehenderit in voluptate velit esse molestaie consequat, vel illum dolore eu fugiat nulla pariatur.

At vero eos et accusam et iusto odium dignissim qui blandit praesent luptatum delenit aigue duos dolor et se molestias excepteur sint occaecat cupidat non provident, simil sunt in culpa qui officia deserunt mollit anim id est laborum et dolor fuga. Et harumd dereud facilis est er expedit distinct. Nam liber tempor cumet soluta nobis eligend optio.

Summer season for bats

E vero eos et accusam et iusto odium dignissim qui blandit praesent luptatum delenit aigue duos dolor et se molestias excepteu sint occaecat cupidat non provident, simil sunt in culpa qui officia deserunt mollit anim id est laborum et dolor fuga. Et harumd dereud facilis est er expedit distinct. Nam liber tempor cumet soluta nobis eligend optio.

Advertising: CLIENT PRESENTATIONS

As your campaign takes shape you will need to consider how to display and present your work. TV advertisements, whether lasting five seconds or sixty, are often worked up into a sequential set of visuals. Storyboard pads, as they are known, are available at graphics suppliers and will assist in the layout of a TV campaign. The page is divided into segments representing individual picture frames. Below each of these, key parts of the script or sound effects can be indicated. It is not necessary to illustrate the entire commercial.

Press advertisements need to be visualized to actual finished size. There are a number of ways you can present these, ranging from actually pasting them into the publication, to displays on flip charts. The advantage of flip charts is that you can prepare a number of "pages," each one illustrating in a sequence an advertisement from your campaign, so that you can show the campaign unfolding.

Agencies often go to great lengths to present the work of the creative team. With TV concepts they may put together a mock advertisement using video techniques or creating film stills, known as animatics. These stills are rendered as marker visuals, put on film, and run through on a screen to represent the action of the TV commercial.

The key medium to master is the marker pen; you should be able to use these with confidence and skill. They are most useful for jotting down ideas quickly in the form of roughs. Their range of thicknesses will give you everything from bold images to light representations. You can render type heavily or lightly, and with flat colors and tones give body and form to a visual.

Markers can be used later in a more precise way to create mock-ups and visuals. Simulated photographic subjects can be suggested in highly realistic form, and

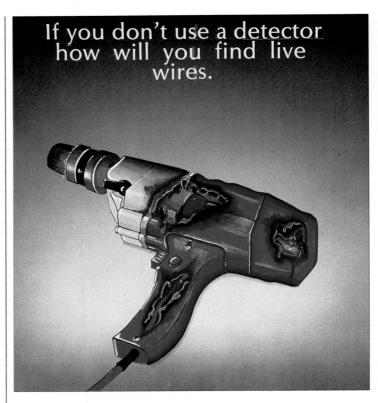

■ **Marker visuals** The illustration for this advertisement has been created using markers to simulate a photograph. The client had to be able to identify this when the visual was presented. The type has been overlaid using acetate and white rub-down lettering.

■ **Collage** This presentation consists of collaged elements. The illustrations were mounted on the background paper. The type was then photocopied onto film and positioned over the elements.

■ **Photocopies and color film** Photocopies can be used for background effects and illustrations in your presentations. These can be colored using film or can be added to using a color copier, or simply copied on colored paper. White-out text can be placed on film and integrated into the photocopying process.

type such as text or headings indicated with accuracy and detail. In fact, marker pens can be used to take the basis of an idea through to a highly realistic representation of the finished job. These simple techniques are applied to all advertising material from press advertisements, to TV storyboards, to leaflets, posters, and even brochures.

The advertising agency's creative team is at the forefront of modern methods for generating graphic imagery, particularly when it comes to advertising. Computers play an important role in exploring and inventing new visuals, and this growing technology has enabled innovative imagery to be shown on the small screen.

Our overheads are greater than other shops.

Shopping shouldn't cost the earth

■ **Black and white** Powerful black and white images (left) can be achieved with markers or photocopied simulations Mechanical tints can be introduced to give tonal effects. The brochure (below) uses space to give the visuals impact and power.

Now instant cash means you don't have to give up your interest.

Whatever method for instant cash you'd used in the past, the likelihood would have been that you would have ended up paying the penalty for it. This could have ranged from the pawning of an intended engagement ring, to the loss of interest from your high interest account.

But now, with the introduction of our Liquid Gold Account, you can get the benefit of a higher rate of interest, with the bonus of being able to withdraw your money instantly, without suffering any penalties. For further information complete the coupon, and return it FREEPOST to the address below.

NAME ....
ADDRESS ....

LEEDS PERMANENT
BUILDING SOCIETY
Head Office: Permanent House,
The Headrow, Leeds LS1 1NS

the Leeds
LIQUID GOLD

INSTANT ACCESS, NO PENALTIES

Alternatives to our high interest account often carry penalties.

the Leeds
LIQUID GOLD

INSTANT ACCESS, NO PENALTIES

T I P S

■ Find the right medium for your presentation.
■ Color photographs can be represented using professional marker pens.
■ Elements can be brought together in a presentation by careful and accurate cutting and assembling.
■ Photocopying on colored papers can be effective.
■ Photocopying type on acetate makes an effective overlay.
■ Black and white advertisements need careful use of tone. Think positively in black and white.

Critique

The first assignment was to produce a strong press campaign for the client, Parents for Safe Food. Two avenues were used by the students. A series of black and white advertisements pinpointed the dangers of irradiation, pesticides, and chemical additives. The advertisement shown here clearly describes the effects irradiation has on food and delivers a shock by deliberate exaggeration of the visual image. The text supporting the advertisement is precise and authoritative.

The next campaign was a series of posters for outsize male fashions. The students first investigated the use of headings and visual images to create verbal and visual puns. The students then became aware that the visual strength of the campaign was more powerful than the headlines. The strapline — common to all the posters — for this campaign was then given greater prominence in the visuals. The advertisement shown here explores the visual presentation, with a striking image touched with humor.

The project to devise a point of sale device looked for a way of incorporating an advertisement into a sales dispenser. The formula used to solve the wrapping paper problem has many merits but it would need a further display panel. The label device works well in describing price and qualities, but these would be difficult to see in a busy Post Office. The construction of the model would also need simplification to be produced economically. However, the concept works and is simple and original.

The final piece is the finished folder for the English Gardening School. The folder idea fulfilled the assignment in many ways: it satisfied the client's preference for retaining the school's typeface and accommodated this in an innovative way. The folder also made a presentation pack.

How many times have you been told to wash fruit before you eat it. Unfortunaly washing will only clean the surface. But an apple will soak up pesticide like a sponge, just as you will when you eat the apple. A typical English apple wil be sprayed 12 times before you or your child eats it. If that wasn't reason enough not to buy one, consider that 22% of pesticides are known or suspected carcinogens (cancer inducing). In the U.S.A. 1 in every 1000 children have contracted cancer from eating pesticide ridden fruit. At Parents For Safe

When pesticides are sprayed on to fruit it doesn't just stay on the surface.

Food we want to make sure action is taken, before our children contract cancer. Like you, we are concerned about the safety of our childrens food, and we have good reason to be. The food industry, scientific advisors and even the government admit that some of the food we eat is unsafe. We will insist that they put health and safety before profit. If you would like to become a Parent For Safe Food yourself or just require more information on the subject we will be pleased to hear from you. Contact Parents For Safe Food, Britannia House, Hammersmith, London W6 0LF

P A R E N T S   F O R   S A F E   F O O D

■ **Press advertisements** The black and white advertisement (above) is one of a series of concepts produced for Parents for Safe Food. Each of the advertisements covers an aspect of suspect treatment of food. The visual layout and typestyles are retained in each advertisement with marker illustrations indicating eventual photography.

■ **Posters** The finished visuals for High and Mighty are simple and clean with punchy illustrations which could either be drawn naturalistically or photographed from made up models. The typeface and the use of gold on the type soften the humorous aspect of the illustrations. The juxtaposition of witty image and subtle typography creates an

atmosphere of class and sophistication.

HIGH & MIGHTY
Quality clothes for large men

■ **Mailers** The project (below) was actually printed for the client. The color for the folder was altered from green to gray with "The English Gardening School" printed in dark gray. Various leaflets were produced to be inserted in the folder.

■ **Point of sale** The final display model (right) shows effectively the type of structure and modeling of this free standing dispenser. For this to be produced commercially some of the elements would need surface printing rather than the use of elaborate labels and strings.

1990
GARDEN VISITS

1990
GARDEN VISITS

The gardens we have chosen are notable for their design and their planting. Those we have already visited we are returning to at a different season. In all cases the coach will leave the Chelsea Physic Garden at 9.30 am **sharp** and return here at approximately 6.30 pm. Please try not to plan anything for the early evening immediately after the tour as the traffic occasionally prevents a prompt return. Sue MacDonald and/or Rosemary Alexander will accompany each group and explain the planting and design. Notes about the gardens will be supplied and there may be an opportunity to buy plants.

The cost of the day is £49.45 including VAT and includes transport by coach to and from the School, entry to each garden, coffee and tea and a picnic lunch with wine.

CONCLUSION

As you progress toward becoming a graphic designer you will have realized that many factors contribute to your success.

This book should have made you aware of many of the development stages you will encounter. The experiments in the early part will have led you to the media you favor, which should help you express yourself in a new and fulfilling way. Each technique mastered will assist you in the process of putting ideas on paper.

You should have learned discipline in generating ideas and should now realize that there is such an abundance of visual information available that ideas can always be found. By now you should be enjoying the process of manipulating graphic elements within a space and seeking out how best they can be used. As you learn, your work should improve all the time.

Do not expect to be a graphic designer as soon as you close this book. This is just the beginning of your future in this creative business.

Your portfolio should reflect your understanding and effort. Once you have learned both to develop and to express ideas you will be in a position to seek professional judgment of your work.

If your ideas are good and your work reflects this with vitality you will eventually succeed. You may find the first studio you try is highly critical of your

■ **Above** An experimental drawing from Chapter One.

■ **Above** Type images used as decorative statements.

■ **Below** An exercise in three-dimensional graphics from Chapter Two.

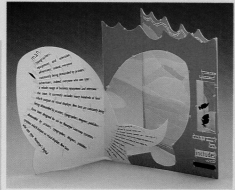

approach to graphics. Do not be deterred. Your work may not fit in with their style. There is bound to be one that will want to take you on.

Remember, graphic design is about vision, ideas, and the future. Some studios will be interested only in fitting you into the current system. Designers with greater vision will realize that you are the future of the industry.

There is no one correct formula for producing work described in this book. Each page offers advice and practical help. It is for you to interpret for yourself the way you explore the processes.

Look at your work carefully. Be your own judge and jury. Once you are able to be self-critical you will understand your strengths and weaknesses. If you can then build on your strengths you will fulfil your ambitions.

■ **Above** A visual for an advertising project.

■ **Right** A packaging design from Chapter Three.

INDEX

CREDITS

Quarto would like to thank the following for their help with this publication and for permission to reproduce copyright material. Whilst every effort has been made to trace and acknowledge all copyright holders, Quarto would like to apologize if any omissions have been made.

Key
a = above
b = below
r = right
fr = far right
l = left
fl = far left
c = center
t = top
bt = bottom

Abbreviations for colleges
AC = The American College in London
BC = Barnet College
BUC = Buckinghamshire College of Higher Education
CC = Croydon College
EC = Ealing College
EPC = Epping College
KI = Kent Institute of Art and Design
NC = Newham Community College

p12 J. Gahir (NC)
p13 D. Ferry (Lecturer, KI)
p15 l. D. Ferry (Lecturer, KI); r J. Gahir (NC)
p16 J. Gahir (NC)
p17 M. Yeo (NC)
p18–19 J. Gahir (NC)
p20–21 E. Jones (Lecturer, CC)
p22 R. Calder (NC), S. Gahir (NC), C. Sparks (NC), W. Francis (NC)
p23 fr M. Ashen (EPC)
p25 bt, fr A. Hayden (EPC)
p26–27 t A. Swann;
p27 fr A. Hayden (EPC)
p28 A. Swann
p29 C. Sukuraman (NC)
p31 A. Antoniou (NC)
p32–33 C. Sukuraman, A. Antoniou (NC)
p35 M. Yeo (NC)
p36–37 C. Sukuraman, A. Antoniou (NC)
p38 1–4 C. Sukuraman (NC); 5–8 A. Hayden (EPC);
p39 9–13 P. Tickner (EPC); 14–16 A. Swann
p42 I. Phillips (NC)
p43 J. Smith (EC)
p44–45 A. Swann

p46 t A. Swann; b Bob Cotton (Lecturer, NC)
p47 A. Swann
p48 b A. Antoniou (NC)
p49 br P. Duffy (Lecturer, EPC)
p50–53 R. Calder (NC)
p54–55 A. Button (Lecturer, NC)
p59 fr A. Swann
p60 T. Holmes (EPC)
p61 tl F. McSweeney (NC); tr M. Hayden (EPC); bl A. Antoniou (NC); br T. Maitland (NC)
p62–63 A. Antoniou (NC)
p64–65 M. Ashen (EPC)
p68–69 C. Sukuraman (NC)
p70 M. Jean-Marie (NC)
p71 M. Jean-Marie (NC); r S. Petrie (NC)
p72 M. Yeo, A. Antoniou (NC)
p73 J. Ferdinand (EPC)
p74–75 J. Ferdinand (EPC)
p77 BC
p78–79 NC
p80–81 H. Flora (NC)
p82–83 BC
p84 l A. Swann; r J. Ferdinand (EPC)
p85 J. Ferdinand (EPC)
p86–87 M. Gudlaughsson (AC)
p88–89 L. Hayden (NC)
p90–93 K. Lee (NCC)
p94–95 J. Ferdinand (EPC)
p96–97 B. Hayden, R. Calder, D. Hales, I. Phillips (NC)
p98–99 J. Ferdinand (EPC)
p101 l A. Antoniou (NC); r J. Ferdinand (EPC)
p102–103 J. Ferdinand (EPC)
p105 P. Duffy (Lecturer, EPC)
p106–109 A. Swann, B. Cotton (Lecturer, NC)
p112–114 Ian Logan
p116–119 M. Hughes (EPC)
p120–129 S. Bridges, E. Bennett, J. Salinger (NC)
p130–133 Colin McHenry
p134–137 J. Ferdinand (EPC)
p138–147 P. Stitson, B. Griver, J. Salinger (NC)
p148–153 T. Holmes, B. Griver (NC)
p158–165 S. Bridges, T. Cox, J. Salinger (NC)
p166–169 Billy Mawhinney
p170–175 A. Rowbury, S. Chamberlain (BUC)
p176–177 S. Lewin (NC)
p178–181 A. Swann
p182–183 A. Rowbury, S. Chamberlain (BUC)
p184–185 tl and tr A. Rowbury, S. Chamberlain (BUC); bl S. Lewin (NC); br A. Swann
p186–187 t H. Flora (NC); m A. Rowbury, S. Chamberlain (BUC); b NC

192